Learning Shooting Sports

Archery, Rifle, Pistol

Katrin Barth & Beate Dreilich

Sports Science Consultant:
Dr. Berndt Barth

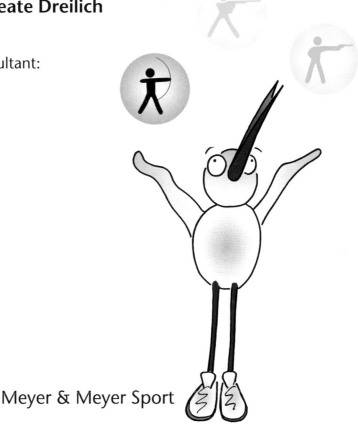

Meyer & Meyer Sport

Original title: Ich lerne Sportschießen
© 2009 by Meyer Meyer Verlag
Translated by Petra Haynes
AAA Translation, St. Louis, Missouri, USA
www.AAATranslation.com

Learning Shooting Sports

© 2010 by Meyer & Meyer Sport (UK) Ltd.
Aachen, Adelaide, Auckland, Budapest, Capetown, Graz, Indianapolis,
Maidenhead, Olten (CH), Singapore, Toronto
Member of the World
Sports Publishers' Association (WSPA)
www.w-s-p-a-org
Printed and bound by: B.O.S.S Druck und Medien GmbH
ISBN 978-1-84126-294-9
E- Mail: info@m-m-sports.com
www.m-m-sports.com

. . . TABLE OF CONTENTS

Please note:

The exercises and practical suggestions in this book have been carefully chosen and reviewed by the authors. However, the authors are not liable for accidents or damages of any kind incurred in connection with the content of this book.

For the purpose of better readability, we have decided to use only the male (neutral) form of address throughout the book, which of course also includes the female gender. This book has been thoroughly edited. However, all of the information is subject to correction.

 Would you like to color the picture? If this book is yours, then pick up your crayons and get started! Finish the drawing!

1 Dear Shooting Athletes

Was it your parents, your friends, the well-known sports shooting club in your area or the television coverage of the world championships or the Olympics? It doesn't really matter how you became interested in shooting sports – you chose a great sport!

You are probably interested in technical things, are good at concentrating and like to spend time with other athletes. With lots of patience and perseverance you will soon achieve your goal. And then you will be very proud of yourself!

In this children's book about shooting sports we have compiled lots of interesting facts about your favorite sport. We give you the most important information about the gear, how to handle the sports equipment, beginning techniques, how to practice, and how to avoid mistakes.

9

Are shooting sports right for you?

Here are some reasons why children enjoy shooting sports. Which ones apply to you? Check "YES" or "NO"

	Yes	No
I love sports.	☐	☐
I like being with other children.	☐	☐
I am interested in technical things.	☐	☐
I am good at concentrating.	☐	☐
I am happy when I achieve goals.	☐	☐
I want to learn about my body.	☐	☐
My family or friends also practice shooting sports.	☐	☐
I want to improve my willpower and courage.	☐	☐
I want to learn something special not everyone can do.	☐	☐
I want to be better than the others.	☐	☐
I want to be in the newspaper.	☐	☐
I want to be successful and famous some day.	☐	☐

If you answered most of these questions with "YES", you have chosen the right sport! Maybe you will be a successful shooter some day.

Maybe some day you will be a member of a successful national team. You will get the highest scores and win championships and medals. But even if shooting remains just a nice recreational activity, you will have a lot of fun and it will keep your body and mind fit and healthy.

This little book is intended to be your companion in shooting sports. We may view something differently from the way your coach, trainer or an experienced shooter explains it – that can happen sometimes. Just ask questions. Even in shooting sports opinions sometimes differ.

When we refer to shooters, trainers, coaches, referees, etc., we of course are not just talking about men and boys, but also about all women and girls.

Have fun with shooting sports!
Sammy and the authors.

In this book you will often see some pictures of Sammy the stork.

This symbol means that Sammy has a tip for you. He points out mistakes you can avoid or gives you advice.

Pretty tricky! Sometimes Sammy has a task or a puzzler for you. You will find these next to the question mark.

The answers and solutions are in the back of the book.

Pretty handy – Sammy can write with his beak! Wherever you see him writing, there is a place for you to record, fill in or color something.

You can use this book as a training diary. Record your progress and your goals. When you have become an experienced shooter, you can enjoy reading about how it all began. If you like, you can add photos of yourself or your friends and collect autographs.

Here Sammy shows you some exercises you can do outside of your training session. Of course they are not a substitute for your training, but they are a good addition. Maybe your friends, siblings or parents will even join in.

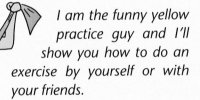

I am the funny yellow practice guy and I'll show you how to do an exercise by yourself or with your friends.

And I am the little blue mistake guy. I deliberately make mistakes – only to help you, of course! Let's see if you can recognize them all. If you're not sure, check the solution pages.

Here is a place where you can paste a nice photo of yourself.

. . . . 2 How Shooting Sports Began

Weapons have always been of great importance to people. They use them to hunt and to make war. But they also enjoy the beauty of the skill-at-arms and compete against each other in competitions.

Hunting for food

Weapons have always been needed to hunt and kill animals. People needed rabbits, buffalo, birds, fish and many other species as important food sources. In the Stone Age, hunting weapons were bifaces and spears made from stone with wooden grips. Later, there were axes and knives, as well as spear tips made of iron. After the invention of gunpowder, hunters were able to kill their prey from a greater distance with their firearms.

Defense

Especially people living in remote areas must protect their families and possessions from attacks by wild animals. People arm themselves to stave off an attack. Unfortunately there have also always been people who fought each other and waged wars.

Competitions

Whoever handles the weapon most skillfully and comfortably is admired, cheered and celebrated. That is why competitions have always been staged where the best could demonstrate their weapon skills and compete against each other.

15

Development of weapons

Weapons of Stone Age man

The first weapons humans hunted and fought with were probably made from flint. The sharply tapered stone wedge was used to kill and skin animals as well as for defense. The stone wedges were held by hand or mounted on sticks.

Metal weapons

Copper and bronze were discovered approximately 5000 years ago. This new material offered many more options for arrow and spear points, knives, axes, lances and swords.

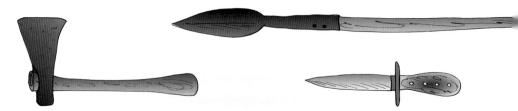

Even during the Ice Age, armorers did not only pay attention to the weapons' superior performance but also to their beauty. Many weapons were adorned with ornate decorations and engravings.

Longbow and crossbow

The longbow and crossbow were developed from the simple bow during the Middle Ages. The string on the crossbow could be made so taut with a mechanical clamping system that it had a very wide range. However, the cocking process also took longer. In comparison, the longbow did not go as far but the rate of fire was much quicker. Most armies therefore chose both weapons.

Firearms

Gunpowder was invented in Europe, in the 14th century, and initially was used in large cannons. Only in the 16th century was gunpowder used for handguns. The wooden grip made aiming easier, it could absorb the recoil and the shooter did not burn his hand on the hot barrel.

17

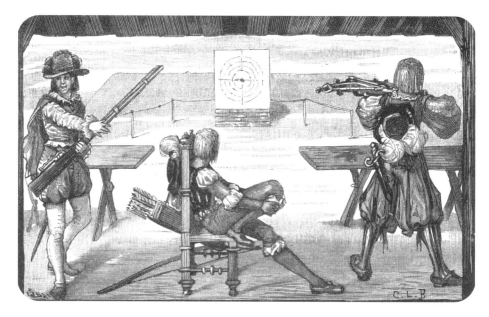

Weapons as sports equipment

Many of the tools people used for hunting, self-defense or fighting later developed into sports equipment. Competitions would determine who was most skillful at handling slingshots, spears, sabers, bows or firearms.

Shooting athletes built competition sites with firing positions, targets and safety zones. Rules of competition were established and referees were chosen. The shot's objective is to hit the bull's-eye, and of course to do so as often as possible.

Modern laser light weapons are safe and can even be used by younger shooting athletes for training and competition.

Organizations for shooting athletes in the United States

USA Shooting (USAS) was chartered by the United States Olympic Committee as the national governing body for the sport of shooting in April 1995. It is headquartered in Colorado Springs, Colorado, at the U.S. Olympic Training Center, and has approximately 5000 members.

Youth Shooting Athletes

The National 4-H Shooting Sports Foundation works with the International Hunter Education Association (IHEA) and USA Shooting. The focus of this program is the development of youth as individuals by helping them learn to shoot, and teaching them the safe and responsible use of firearms, and the principles of hunting and archery.

If you want to know more, check out the Internet at www.usashooting.com or www.IHEA.com.

Organisations for shooting athletes in the United Kingdom

The National Small-bore Rifle Association was founded in 1901 and is the National Governing Body for smallbore shooting. It is based at Bisley, Surrey and has a membership of about 6,000 individuals and over 1,000 clubs and associations.

NSRA Olympic disciplines
Rifle
Pistol

Other disciplines
Crossbow
Sporter air rifle

Young Shooters
The NSRA's Youth Proficiency Scheme provides a framework through which young people have the opportunity to take up target shooting. The

19

scheme can be run within a shooting club, but is also used by many youth organisations such as the Scout Association, the Cadet Forces and schools.

To find more information or a club go to **www.nsra.co.uk**.

RIFLE-PISTOL	ARCHERY
National Small-bore Rifle Asssociation, Lord Roberts Centre, Bisley Camp, Brookwood, Woking, Surrey GU24 0NP www.nsra.co.uk http://www.nsra.co.uk Tel 01483 485503	**The Grand National Archery Society,** Lilleshall National Sports Centre, Newport, Shropshire, TF10 9AT www.gnas.org.uk http://www.gnas.org.uk

Pictograms

Surely you have seen different sports depicted as drawings or symbols on television, in the newspaper, on stickers or posters. These symbols are called **pictograms**. The drawing is very simple, yet everyone immediately recognizes the correct sport.

Here you can see such a pictogram for shooting sports.

. . . . 3 Hi There, Ralf Schumann!

Born: June 10, 1962 in Meissen, Germany
Occupation: Sheet metal worker, precision mechanic, trainer
Height/weight: 5'6"/159 lbs
Sporting firearm: Rapid fire pistol
Titles: 3 x Olympic Champion, 2 x Olympic Silver Medalist, 4 x World Champion, 13 x Overall World Cup Winner, 39 x World Cup Winner

It's so great that you are letting us do an interview! How did you actually get involved with sports shooting?

My school offered lots of opportunities for learning different sports, such as air rifle shooting. Unfortunately I was too small for that. The coaches were concerned that I might injure my back and so I was not allowed to participate. But I kept going back. Then I got permission to shoot an air pistol and actually scored a hit. I had found the right one!

What do you think is so great about shooting sports?

As a little boy, I played cowboy and I pretended to shoot at everything with a "Bang!" But the question remained whether I would have hit anything! That continues to be the challenge: Can I shoot with such concentration and precision that I will hit the 10? Over and over again, and many times in a row?

What was your greatest / most important success?

I could list many different successes. The beginning was great, always hitting the big target and even hitting the mark with every shot. In time more of the holes were in the center and I even won some competitions. Then the best and most important successes are achieving the goals you have set for competitions. That includes the first medals in the German National Championships, the European Championships, the World Championships, the Olympics, and then of course the first gold medals.

You have already won many international titles. Do you have any more athletic ambitions?

Yes, I do have more athletic goals! After I had at some point won all the individual medals I tried to repeat them all and get higher scores.

Which talents must a good shooter have?

Most important to me is when the joy and the desire to practice shooting sports are really huge. It is also good for a shooter to have enough strength to hold the firearm, healthy eyes, sensitive hands and quiet hands.

Do you sometimes not feel like practicing? What do you do?

That happens sometimes. Then I think about the goal I have set for myself and I know that I have to train for that. Sometimes the training exercises are really not fun, but I know that they are an important part of the training and that I have to get past this situation and master it. It can happen sometimes that there is a competition on a day I'm not feeling so hot. Then I can say to myself: "I've experienced this in training and I worked through it just fine!"

How do you stay fit?

I really enjoy bicycling, running, walking and inline skating. That's good for overall fitness. I don't do too much weight lifting with heavy weights because it makes the hands less steady. I use smaller weights for a variety of exercises.

What is the best way for you to concentrate?

I can concentrate best when I am able to stay calm and focus on whatever I have to do at that moment. That can be individual segments of a motion sequence or entire processes or series of shots. It is important to have your mind completely on the things you are practicing at that moment.

What are your interests? What do you do in your free time?

I like to spend my free time with my wife and friends from my community. I also enjoy spending time in our garden, which lies at the edge of a creek. There I am able to really relax.

Do you have any tips for young shooting athletes?

Enjoy your sport and be persistent in pursuing the goals you have set. Don't give up! Treat your shooting equipment with care and always observe the safety rules on the shooting range!

*Have fun training
and God bless!*

23

Fan page

My favorite shooting athlete:

_____

Biggest successes:

_____

_____

Photos and newspaper clippings

Here you can collect autographs from successful shooting athletes or paste photos.

Each target appears only once in each color in every row, column and diagonal. Draw the remaining targets in the appropriate colors in the correct locations!

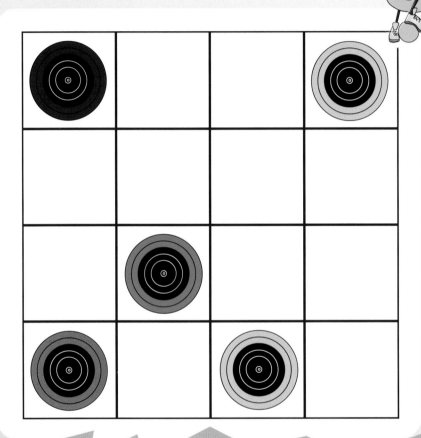

Tina watches Julie at the shooting range.
She asks: "I guess you like shooting?"
"Sure!" answers Julie. "Then why don't you learn how to do it?"

The coach asks Tom: "Why do you come to practice with dirty hands?"
Answers Tom: "I don't have any others!"

. . . . . 4 No Pain, No Gain

Surely you have dreamt about what it would be like to be the best. Everyone cheers you on, is in awe of and admires you. You are shooting with concentration, error-free and get the highest scores. The fans assail you and want your autograph. And then you accept the good wishes of your teammates, your coach, your fans, your friends and your parents …!

But stop! Just lying in the grass dreaming of success isn't enough!

If you want to be a good shooter, maybe even better than the others, you have to practice often and diligently. That's not always easy and isn't always fun right away.

Shhh! He's asleep and dreaming of his big win!

Remember:
Diligence leads to success!

27

Goals are important

When you begin shooting sports, you must ask yourself the following questions:

What is my goal?

Just raising the sporting firearm or bow, taking aim and "blasting away" is fun, but not for long! You want to be able to aim more calmly and with more concentration as well as more accuracy. Maybe you'll start at the national championships some day or eventually make the national team.

Of course you are still too young for that. But nevertheless, you should already have some bigger goals now. You have to know what you want. If you don't have a goal, practicing soon won't be fun anymore. So you continue to set bigger goals. That's what the successful top shooters do, too!

There are the "small" and near goals:
To be commended at the next practice session or to finally be able to place the shots in a tight group.

There are also more distant goals:
To soon be able to coordinate taking aim and pulling the trigger, or rather to take aim and release, or to make the top five at the next competition.

And of course many shooting athletes have the ultimate goal:
To eventually get high ring scores or point scores and win medals at the World Championships and the Olympics.

Why did you become a shooting athlete? What are your goals? What do you want to achieve?

_____

_____

How do I reach my goal?

You want to accomplish a lot, but how can you achieve your goals? Definitely by practicing lots and lots! But add to that the necessary concentration exercises, technique training, as well as the endurance and strength exercises the coach will go through with you. There will most certainly be some things you won't enjoy very much. Some things may seem boring and much too strenuous. But all of these exercises will help you achieve your goals.

How often do I need to practice?

It's just like everything else in life – only those who work hard will be successful! And how does it work that you get better and better with lots of practice? As long as the exercises are easy and relaxed, you will only do what you already know. Only when something is strenuous and you really have to concentrate are you getting better.

That means you have to work hard and put in lots of effort to make progress. When you haven't been to shooting practice for a while, you will notice that you have gotten a little worse and aren't as calm and focused and accurate. Now you have to catch up!

The more diligently and frequently you practice, the better you will be!

29

Physical fitness is important

Phew! I can't go on! I'm wiped out!

Oh no! What's wrong with Sammy? The competition just started and he's already totally anxious and exhausted! Has that ever happened to you? Do you also lose your concentration and nerve that easily? Then you need to work on your **fitness level**!

What should a shooting athlete be able to do particularly well? Cross out the things that are less important. If we forgot anything, write it down!

Run fast

Play flute

Jump

Ski

Stand up straight without wobbling

See well

Good with mechanical things

Good concentration

Good observer

Can do sports for an hour

Throw accurately

Change running speed

Tell jokes

What is physical fitness?

Since shooting is not a sport in which the athlete does endurance running, jumps far, or does quick somersaults, some may think that physical fitness isn't that important. But on the contrary: physical fitness is very important!

What do you need?

You need good **endurance** to handle physical exertion for an extended period of time. Then you won't get winded so fast when running, jumping, bicycling or swimming. You'll have more staying power while shooting and you will recover quickly and feel fit again.

If you want to be able to stand for a long period of time, hold the bow, the pistol or the rifle steadily and always keep your balance at the same time, you need strong muscles. Arm **strength**, as well as strong hands and fingers are also important so you can hold and operate your piece of equipment accurately.

In addition it is also important for a shooting athlete to be able to react instantly to the correct target. That requires **speed**, especially in your head and fingers.

Agility is important for an optimal body position while taking aim, so head, shoulders, hips and feet can be in proper alignment with each other.

Your training will not only take place at the shooting range. Your coach will most certainly do a number of other aiming and scoring games, running exercises, fitness exercises, and much more. Really participate because all of these things are great for your physical fitness level.

31

This is how you can practice

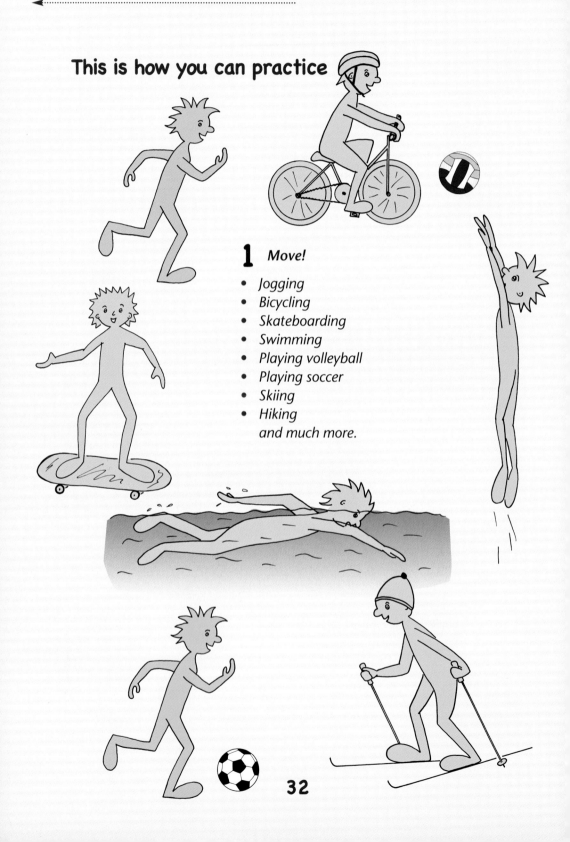

1 *Move!*

- *Jogging*
- *Bicycling*
- *Skateboarding*
- *Swimming*
- *Playing volleyball*
- *Playing soccer*
- *Skiing*
- *Hiking*
  and much more.

2 *Fast and agile*

- **Slalom run**
  Set up a slalom course using poles, cones or other objects.
  Run through it without making mistakes and keep trying
  to lower your time.

- **High and low**
  Set up a course with several low hurdles in a row. The
  runner jumps over the first hurdle, crawls under the next
  hurdle, jumps over the one after that, etc..

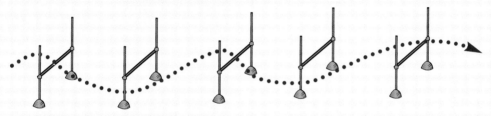

3 *Balance and dexterity*

- **Keeping your balance**
  Try balancing on one leg for an extended period of
  time. As you do so, sing a song, clap your hands, make
  faces or silly movements.

- **Balancing**
  Balance your way along a chalk line or a beam. You may be able
  to find some low walls in your neighborhood or some logs in the
  woods to balance on.

- **Dexterity exercises**
  Many athletic exercises require a good sense of balance and skill. Try
  inline skating, ice skating, walking on stilts, riding a mountain bike
  or a unicycle. Have you ever juggled?

Which sport other than shooting do you enjoy?

33

Everything packed?

You are very excited because you are going to an out-of-town competition. You practiced lots and the team lineup is set. But imagine you arrive at the competition site, stand at the shooting stand, unpack your gym bag, and … where are your shoes? Your well broken-in "super competition shoes" are at home – far away! Just plain forgotten! There is no one to borrow shoes from, and they wouldn't fit you properly anyway. The fact that you don't feel comfortable now while taking aim is your problem alone and of course really aggravating.

Your parents could of course help pack your bag, but every shooting athlete is responsible for making sure that his own equipment is complete and neat.

The checklist

Many athletes know that anxious feeling of forgetting something for practice or an important competition. That is why it is important to prepare everything ahead of time. Pack your gym bag the night before so you can go to bed with your mind at ease.

Many athletes have found the checklist to be useful. You write down everything you want to bring along. Anything that's packed is checked off. Use a pencil so you can erase the checks for the next time you pack.

My checklist

☐ Jacket

☐ Pants

☐ Warm Underwear

☐ Athletic Shoes

☐ Headband

☐ Blinder

☐ _____

☐ _____

☐ _____

☐ _____

☐ _____

☐ _____

☐ _____

☐ _____

Use the blank lines to write down anything else you can't forget.

1 *Which thrower will hit the stack of cans?*

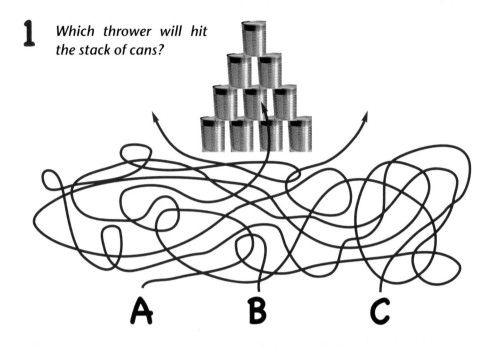

A   B   C

2 *At a festival the children were allowed to throw letters off a wall. What was the word the competitors "shot down"?*

. . . . 5 Eyes on Target

Can knockdown, target throw, mini golf, bowling, balloon pop... , – there are so many games that require good eyes and steady hands. Most likely you've already noticed that you do particularly well in those games or have a lot of fun playing them and really want to get better.

For safety reasons, young children are not allowed to practice with actual rifles, pistols or bows. But shooting clubs offer many opportunities to practice aiming and hitting the mark. A calm and relaxed posture, a keen eye and controlled breathing are very important here. Then you will be well prepared when it's time for "the real equipment"!

You will practice these things together with your trainers, coaches and fellow athletes. On the following pages you will find lots of information, useful tips and exercises.

37

◄

The eyes

"Keep your eye on the goal!", "Don't lose sight of your goal!", or "To have sharp eyes." Many phrases suggest that the eyes play an important role in aiming.

When you are at the shooting range, your aim is accurate, your stance is quiet and steady and your breathing is even, – then it's the eyes' turn to do their job!

The dominant eye

When taking aim, it is important to figure out which eye will be focused on the target. Using both eyes simultaneously allows you to see spatially, meaning you can see what is in front and what is behind something. This is very important in everyday life and in shooting sports. That is why both eyes remain open while aiming. However, the non-dominant eye is covered with a blinder to make aiming easier.

How do you figure out which is your "aiming eye"? To do so, focus both eyes on a distant spot. Now extend your arm and cover that spot with your thumb. Then cover one eye with the other hand. If the spot stays behind the thumb, the seeing eye is dominant. If the spot jumps to the side, the covered eye is dominant.

Light and dark

The pupil is not a dark spot but a hole in the iris, the colored area of the eye. Light enters the interior of the eye through this hole.
This pupil has an amazing ability: if the light is very bright, the pupil contracts so only a little light can penetrate. If it is dark, the pupil gets very wide and large. (You can see this in the photo.)

Avoid looking into bright sunlight or lamp light before shooting. It causes the pupils to contract, and when subsequently focusing on the dark target the pupils have to first widen again. This hampers sharp vision.

This is how we see

From the outside we can only see a small portion of the eye. We can see primarily the colored retina and the hole in it. That is the pupil which contracts or widens, depending on the amount of light entering it. But the largest part of the eye is hidden in the eye socket.

The rays of light enter through the pupil and are bundled over the lens behind it. The image is projected onto the retina located in the back of the eyeball. There the image of what we see is still small and upside down. The image is transmitted to the brain via the optic nerve, where it is then interpreted as the actual picture. The curvature of the lens from flat to highly curved can "sharpen" the object, like adjusting a pair of binoculars.

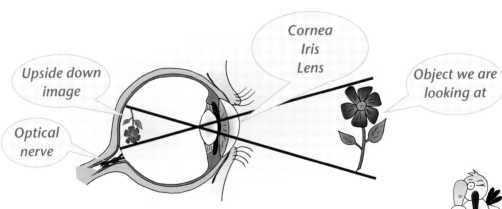

Cornea
Iris
Lens

Upside down image

Object we are looking at

Optical nerve

Carefully feel your eye through your upper lid or gently pull the lower lid down in front of a mirror. You can easily see that the eye is like a ball.

Relaxation and concentration

"Just stay calm! You can do it!" Sounds good but how can you stay calm when you are at an unfamiliar shooting range, you absolutely want to do well and everyone is watching? You start thinking about homework, stress with friends, or anticipating your next birthday party.

Tuning out – it's not that easy!

Sometimes you are relaxed and loose, but sometimes you are definitely anxious, your heart beats fast, the hand shakes and your breathing makes your body tremble. Of course that's not good for a shooting athlete! He must learn to relax and to control his body even in stressful moments.

Shooting sports require composure and concentration. That means your breathing is even and the body stands quietly. Your mind is focused on the task at hand and the rest is blocked out.

But you can't get so calm that you'll almost go to sleep. Your senses should be keen and your vision clear!

Many paths to relaxation

Intending not to think about anything often isn't enough. Lots of thoughts are going around in your head, and they are not that easy to turn off. Most of the time it doesn't work! That's why it is important that you try out what works best for you.

Every shooting athlete has his own way of relaxing! Often it may take a while to find what works best and is most effective for you.

Running away from stress

A good option for relaxation is exercise. It is a way to release tension and fight inner restlessness. But make sure that you don't overdo it right before a practice or competition and as a result end up getting more jumpy.

- Taking a walk
- Jogging
- Dancing
- Biking or inline skating
- Ball games with friends, and much more…!

Quieting down

Additional movement makes some athletes even more restless and fidgety. They should find ways to relax quietly.

- Listening to music
- Reading
- Drinking tea
- Having quiet pleasant conversations
- Relaxation or breathing exercises
- Taking a trip through the body, and much more…!

41

Relaxation and concentration exercises

You know those days when you are just "antsy" and have a hard time concentrating? But for a shooting athlete it is very important to stand very still and hold the sporting firearm or bow without moving. Here are a few relaxation exercises for you.

1 Tree

- *You stand firmly on both feet with your legs closed and look at a distant point. Your arms hang loosely at your sides.*
- *Slowly slide your left foot up the lower right leg. Keep your balance and hold this pose for several breaths.*

2 Flying

- *You stand firmly on both feet with your legs closed and look at a distant point.*
- *As you inhale, lift your arms to the side and lift one knee to the front. Hold this pose for three breaths.*
- *With the third breath, slowly lower your arms and set the foot back down.*
- *Close your eyes and take a deep breath, and repeat this exercise on the opposite side.*

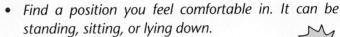

3 Tuning out

- *Find a position you feel comfortable in. It can be standing, sitting, or lying down.*
- *Take a few relaxed breaths.*
- *Close your eyes, cover them with your fingers and close your ears with your thumbs.*
- *"Look" to the inside and take slow even breaths. This is a good way for you to relax.*

4 Triangle

- *Sit upright and relaxed on the front edge of a chair.*
- *Now extend the left leg forward at a slant.*
- *Then place your left hand on your thigh.*
- *The right arm lifts to a horizontal position and then up at a diagonal.*
- *Your eyes are on the extended hand.*
- *Hold this pose for three breaths and then switch sides.*

5 Child's pose

- *Sitting on your heels, fold your torso down and lower your forehead to the floor in front of your knees. The arms rest loosely alongside the body.*
- *Take slow breaths and relax all of your muscles.*

Breathing

The heart beating, swallowing, or blinking your eyelids happen many times a day, even without your having to constantly think about it. Breathing also occurs day and night to keep your body supplied with enough oxygen. But most of the time you breathe without realizing it.

Help! Stop! We only wanted to practice breathing. But that's a hurricane!

But sometimes you feel your breath very intensely: when you are "winded" from running fast, a scare "takes your breath away," or you want to take a really "deep breath" when something smells delicious. Sometimes you have trouble breathing when you have a cold or your clothes are too tight.

Breathing to stay balanced

Breathing is very important to our wellbeing and health. Most of the time, our emotional state can be identified by our breathing. When you are anxious or tense you breathe differently than when you are in a more even and harmonious mood.

When you are anxious, angry or scared, your breathing is quick and flat. The chest rises and flattens more severely and your entire body is restless.

As a shooting athlete, good breathing technique is very important because your breathing helps you with aiming. Anxious breathing and a trembling body are absolutely useless here.

A good shooting athlete is able to "breathe away" his anxiousness by putting particular emphasis on exhaling!

Through the nose, deep into the belly

In every day life we have gotten used to chest breathing. You simply breathe through the mouth and feel your chest expand. But the better and deeper way to breathe is **belly breathing**.

Inhale

- *Inhale preferably only through the nose.*
- *As you do so, the lungs fill with air as you inhale and the diaphragm moves downward.*
- *The stomach becomes convex; only then does the chest rise.*

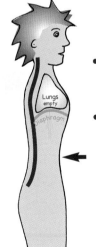

Exhale

- *Exhale through the nose and the slightly open mouth.*
- *First the chest flattens and then the stomach becomes concave.*

Exhaling takes a little longer than inhaling. Wait a few seconds before you take your next breath. Breathe evenly and feel yourself relax.

45

Breathing exercises

To be able to "breathe away" the stress before and during training and competition, you must continue to practice the proper breathing technique.

First practice the difference between chest breathing and belly breathing and feel how your body reacts.

1 **Belly breathing**

Your breath goes into your belly. Can you feel it?

Try it!

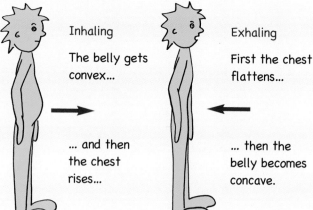

Inhaling

The belly gets convex...

... and then the chest rises...

Exhaling

First the chest flattens...

... then the belly becomes concave.

2 **Chest breathing**

Your breath goes directly into the chest cavity. And the stomach stays flat. Can you feel it?

Try it!

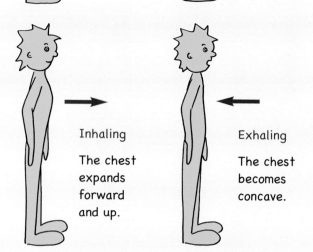

Inhaling

The chest expands forward and up.

Exhaling

The chest becomes concave.

Are you able to think about nothing and just track your breathing? Then you are on the right track! Think about which breathing technique will lead to a more stable stance.

3 *Relaxed belly breathing*

Find a comfortable quiet place where you can relax on your back. You have to feel at ease; make sure where you are lying is not too hard and you are not cold. Take a few minutes to do the following exercise:

- *Close your eyes and place your hands loosely on your stomach.*
- *You are totally relaxed; none of your muscles are tightened.*

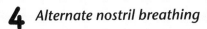

- *You are breathing into your belly, whereby the abdominal wall rises as you inhale and lowers as you exhale.*
- *Breathe as slow or as fast as is natural; do not try to force the pace.*

4 *Alternate nostril breathing*

One very relaxing breathing technique is called alternate nostril breathing. It's not entirely simple, but with a little practice it will become child's play and it feels good.

- *Sit upright and comfortably.*
- *Hold the fingers of your right hand as shown in the illustration. Thumb, ring finger, as well as the pinkie are extended and middle finger and index finger are bent.*

- *Inhale and exhale through only one nostril. The right nostril is closed with the thumb and the left one with the ring finger.*

Always put emphasis on exhaling!

Inhale right – exhale right – short break – switch sides
Inhale left   – exhale left   – short break – switch sides
Inhale right – exhale right – short break – switch sides
Inhale left   – exhale left   – ...

Hit scoring

After shooting, every shooter is eager to know what his shot pattern looks like. The target is scored and each hit is recorded individually. Some you will be happy with and some will make you wonder how they materialized.

You should always be interested in your shooting results. Did you improve? Is there a particular pattern? What can you practice and do better?

Have you noticed that there are specific shot patterns? Often the hits are located in one particular area on the target. This is called a "group." Maybe they are predominantly on the lower part of the target or maybe in the left corner? What does that tell you?

If the hits always deviate in the same direction from the center, you are most likely repeating the same mistake.

Discuss this with your coach. He will most certainly recognize what happened.

Here you can paste your most successful, most interesting, or even your funniest target. You can also draw your hits on this target or take a photo and paste it down.

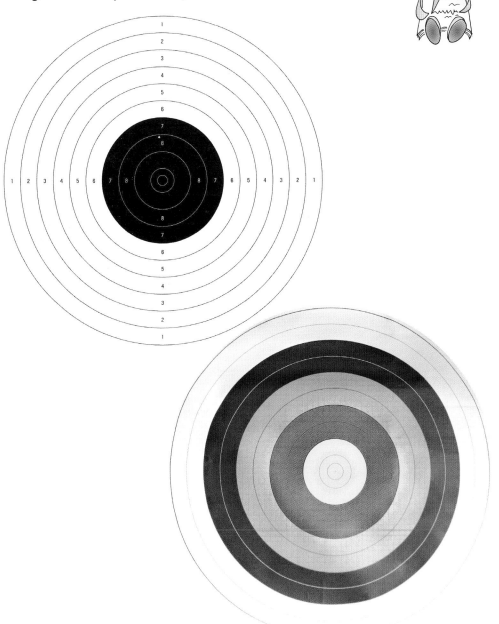

. . . . 6 Archery

When most people think of archery, they probably remember Robin Hood, the "avenger of the poor," or William Tell, the Swiss folk hero. But these two were definitely not the first people to skillfully use bow and arrow.

Bow and arrow were invented as far back as primeval times, which is what researchers found in ancient cave drawings. They date back more than 50,000 years.

Even though the materials have continued to evolve and improve, the bow is still stretched and the arrow is supposed to be shot into the "bull's-eye"!

Shooting range

A shooting range for archery can be on a lawn, in a gymnasium, or at an indoor shooting range. The distance to the firing line is specified in the competition rules. Of course the distance can be changed for beginners or at club competitions to make sure that all archers have fun and are successful. A good starting distance is 5 meters or about 3.5 yards.

Target mats

The target mat is made of plastic or compressed straw. Competitive athletes use pads made from compressed straw particles and a metal core. The size of the pad depends on the faces being used.

Target faces

The size of the fiber-reinforced paper faces depends on the competition and the distance. Two of each white, blue, red and golden rings are marked with the ring numbers 1 to 10. The shot into the "bull's-eye" is rewarded with a 10.

Target stand

The target stand is set up like an easel and has a 15° slant. It supports the target pad.

The circular target pad is made from plastic or compressed straw.

The paper target face is mounted on the target pad.

The yellow-gold circle in the center of the target is every archer's aspiration. Each hit in the center ring is worth 10 points.

The target pad is set up on the portable and stable target stand.

Indoor archery uses short shooting distances. Here an archery safety net should be set up for safety and to protect the arrows.

Bow

Bows are the same as any other sports equipment, – there are the simple ones and also the super-hi-tech apparatuses. Experienced archers often have expensive bows made from fiberglass or carbon. Beginners use simple wooden bows. All bows can be taken apart.

Limbs

The two screw-on limbs are made from wood with a fiberglass laminate coating. During assembly, make sure that the tips of the limbs point in the shooting direction. The locating screws must be firmly tightened.

The riser

The riser for beginners is made from wood or plastic and partially covered with cork or leather. It is easy for the shooter to grip. The arrow rest and the adjustable sight are mounted on the riser.

Bowstring

The bowstring rests in two grooves at each end of the limbs. It consists of many separate strands. In the past they were made from flax, hemp or silk. Today the bowstrings are twisted from synthetic fibers like nylon.

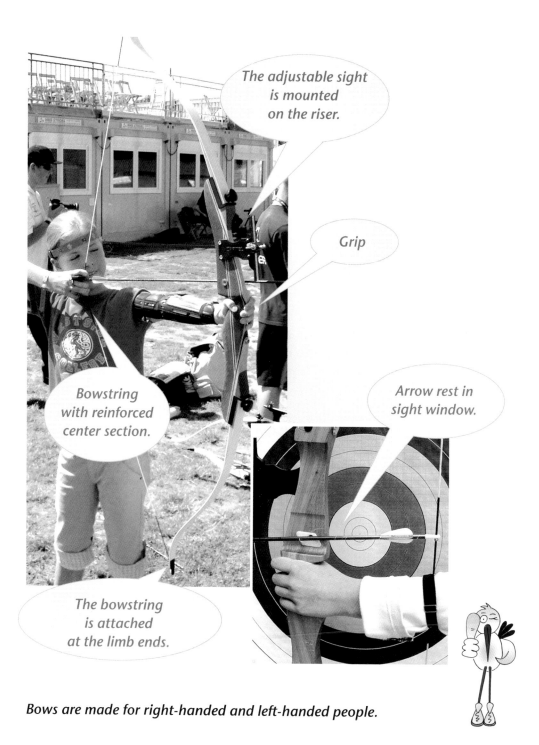

Bows are made for right-handed and left-handed people.

Arrows

What's a bow without arrows? They come in many different lengths, different weights, and are made from different materials. That can be wood, plastic, fiberglass, steel, aluminum or carbon.

The arrow tip is made of metal and at the end of the arrow is the nock. The three feathers stabilize the arrow's flight. They can be real feathers or made from plastic. The arrow is fixed to the bowstring with the aid of a nock groove. The nocking point on the bowstring shows you the best place to do that.

Nock

Feathers

The selection and length of the arrows is not only determined by price, but primarily by the size and ability of the shooter. Your coach will advise you.

Quiver

In order for the arrows not to lie around helter-skelter and to always be handy, they are kept in a quiver. It is worn at your side. Some quivers simply hang from your belt and others come with their own belt.

Always keep three arrows in one opening so you can keep track of your series!

Clothing and equipment

Archers wear normal sportswear like a tracksuit and tennis shoes. This allows for sufficient freedom of movement and a nice solid stance on any surface. Whether indoors or outdoors, the rule of thumb is: dress so you are neither hot nor cold.

Arm protection

The armguard is attached to the lower bow arm and makes sure that the bowstring does not graze the arm when firing. That's because the elbow will protrude into the arrow's firing path if the forearm isn't rotated out properly when the bowstring is cocked. That is pretty painful and of course also alters the arrow's trajectory.

Finger protection

The finger guard, also called a **tap**, makes sure that the three fingers holding the bowstring don't get injured when cocking and releasing the bowstring. Without a tap you quickly get blisters on your fingers. If possible, start out with a tap that has finger separators. The thumb is placed on the thumb rest.

Chest protection

A complete set of protective gear includes a chest guard, which is worn on the side where you hold your bow. When learning the proper technique it can happen that the bowstring grazes the chest while firing. Even top shooters wear this protection, even if they rarely make these types of mistakes anymore.

Archery technique

Right-handed or left-handed?

Before you begin with archery you have to find out if you are right-handed or left-handed. That depends on your dominant eye. (If the right eye is dominant, you cock the bowstring with the right hand!) This puts both eye and bowstring on the same sight line.

You can look up how to determine your dominant eye in the chapter "Eye on Target".

Setting up at the shooting range

When you arrive at the shooting range you first begin to set up.

That includes:

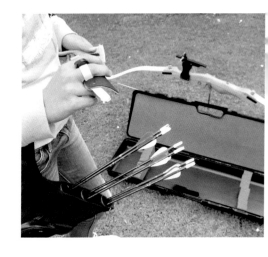

- Assemble the bow (limbs, bowstring, sights).
- Set up bow stand.
- Put on chest guard, arm guard and tap.
- Strap on quiver and fill it with arrows.
- Prepare target face (usually done by the coach).

For safety reasons the bow is cocked only after all shooters and helpers are behind the firing line. Always follow the coaches' orders.

Starting position and preparation

It is crucial that the archer has a firm stance. He must be able to concentrate on the target, calmly cock the bow and release the bowstring without wobbling.

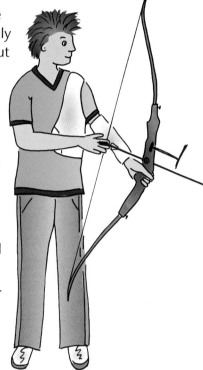

This is what you have to pay attention to:

- The feet are about shoulder-width apart.
- The right-handed archer points his left side to the target.
- Body weight is distributed evenly between both feet.
- The bulk of the weight is on the front and outside edge of the feet.
- You stand at ease and relaxed with your shoulders wide and your back straight.
- Your eyes are on the target so you can focus on the target and the task at hand.

Bow hand

- A right-handed person usually holds the bow with the left hand.
- The bow arm is almost fully extended.
- The fingers hold the grip loosely.
- The wrist is extended and does not move.
- The forearm rotates out while cocking the bowstring.

A bow sling can provide security to keep you from clenching the bow. It prevents the bow from slipping from your hand when you release the bowstring.

59

Drawing fingers

- The bowstring is drawn with the index finger, middle finger and ring finger.
- It lies in the first groove of each finger joint.
- The wrist on the drawing hand is relaxed.

Arrow rest and nocking point

The arrow is placed on the arrow rest with the different-colored feather (cock feather) pointing to the outside, and is clicked into place with the nock above the bowstring's nocking point. This allows the arrow to take off without the feathers scraping along the bow window.

When fitting the arrow, place the index finger of your bow hand on the arrow to keep it from slipping off the arrow rest!

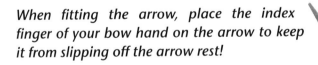

Pre-draw

- To pre-draw, the bowstring is pulled back slightly.
- The head is erect but relaxed, and the eyes are on the target.

- Both bow arm and drawing arm are raised.
- The elbow of the drawing arm is slightly higher than the hand.

Full draw

As the bowstring is drawn, the drawing hand moves close to the body, to the chin.

Anchoring

The bowstring is stretched so far that body and bow form a solid connection.

- The upper edge of the drawing hand is close to the chin below the jaw.
- The head is erect, the mouth closed and the nose makes contact with the bowstring.
- The arrowhead is approximately 2-3 mm from full draw.

Sight adjustment

Now you double check to make sure the sight is in line with the center of the target. If necessary you need to adjust it with a slight movement of your upper body.

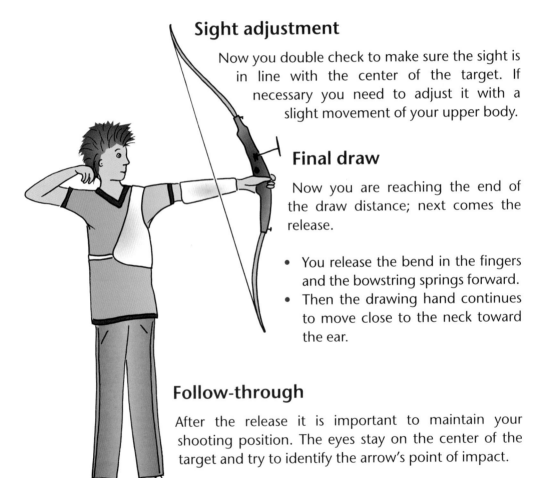

Final draw

Now you are reaching the end of the draw distance; next comes the release.

- You release the bend in the fingers and the bowstring springs forward.
- Then the drawing hand continues to move close to the neck toward the ear.

Follow-through

After the release it is important to maintain your shooting position. The eyes stay on the center of the target and try to identify the arrow's point of impact.

Archery

Aiming and releasing

When aiming, an archer wants to line up four important points on a common sight line:

1 Eye
2 Bowstring shadow
3 Aperture
4 Bull's-eye

Only during the final draw do you watch the sight closely. If the target image is right, the drawing hand opens—release!

Bull's-eye

Aperture

Bow shadow

Eye

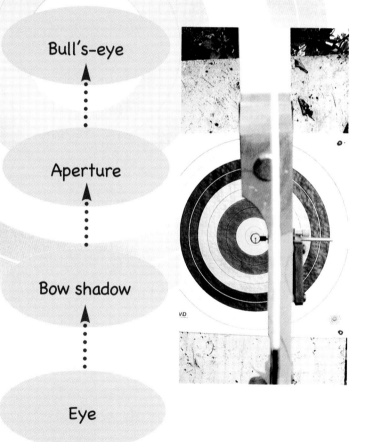

The motion sequence for archery is smooth. There are no breaks between the individual steps. It's just like a song on a CD, where you don't hit the stop button after every line.

Mistakes you need to avoid!

Look at how the little mistake guys practice archery. What are they doing wrong?

1

2

3

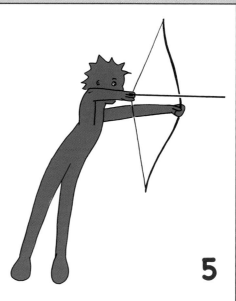

Don't be surprised that these little guys are making such big mistakes! But we had to exaggerate a little to make the mistakes more recognizable. You will find the solutions to the mistakes in the solutions chapter.

Strong back – good posture

Archers really pay attention to good posture because it is the only way to take a successful shot. The back muscles are strengthened during practices and archers rarely have back problems.

There are many exercises for strengthening your back, even outside of scheduled practices. One of them is, for example

"Cow"    "Cat"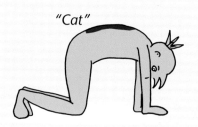

When doing strength exercises make sure that your training isn't one-sided! A strong back needs a strong stomach! That means you definitely need to do abdominal exercises in addition to back exercises.

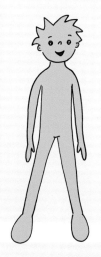

This is how you find the correct shoulder posture

- *You stand in normal position.*
- *The arms hang at your sides.*
- *Your shoulders are down.*
- *Lift the extended arms laterally to shoulder level.*
- *The shoulder girdle is open and wide.*

Get fit with a rubber band

To be able to properly tighten the back muscles, an archer should do supplementary exercises in addition to the regular practice sessions. These include exercises for endurance, strength and agility.

At some point you have surely lifted or pulled something very heavy that made your arms tremble with exertion. That's normal but it can't happen to an archer. That is why you need enough strength in your hands, arms and upper body to take a shot without trembling.

Many archers have found a simple and versatile piece of sports equipment very helpful. The approximately six feet long and six inch wide rubber band is not expensive and doesn't take up much space. It fits into any bag when you travel. The band is available from various manufacturers under different product names.

Arm strengthening exercises

Make sure that your training isn't one-sided, meaning not just one muscle! All of the muscles need to be strengthened!

Strengthening the triceps

- Both arms are extended overhead with the band.

- Now pull the band down on both sides.

Strengthening the biceps

- The band is pinned down in the middle with the foot.

- From a nearly extended position, both arms pull the ends of the band upward.

Strengthening the shoulder muscles

- The feet hold the band in place.
- Now pull the ends of the band up laterally.

Strengthening back and chest muscles

- *The band is stretched across the back.*

- *Forcefully pull the band forward.*

- *Forcefully pull the band upward.*

Cocking the bow

- *You get into a pre-draw position.*
- *When you now move the drawing hand as if to cock the bow, the rubber band is stretched.*
- *Always practice with the other side as well to avoid one-sided workloads.*

To keep the rubber band from slipping out of your hands, you can wrap it around your hand in a loop.

With all of the exercises you have to make sure not to hyperextend your elbows! Don't forget to warm up before practicing!

Learning Shooting Sports

Off to a competition

It is fun to just shoot at the targets. You can work on improving your shooting technique and are happy when you get a hit. But at some point you will want to compete against others and show what you can do at competitions.

Even if competitions for children don't have to be held according to the official rules, it is important that they are fair and that everyone has an even chance.

Important rules are therefore necessary:

- Comparable bow and arrow material (e.g. bows with/without sights)
- Distances to the target
- Number of competition arrows
- Time limit for one round (that's three arrows in a row)
- Age group
- Performance level
- Number of participants
- Allowing handicaps (meaning point advance for weaker participants)

Important safety tips

 Bows and arrows are sports equipment and not toys!

 Always follow the advice of trainers and coaches! The instructions of supervisory personnel must also be followed!

 Make sure that your equipment (clothing, bow, arrows) is in safe condition!

 Wait until it is your turn and the shooting range has been cleared before you fit the arrow!

 You can only shoot in the direction of the target! Do not point the arrow in other directions, and never at people or animals, --not even for fun!

 Always make sure that the range is clear and that no one is standing there!

 Never take an empty shot (meaning pulling the bowstring and releasing it without an arrow)!

 The arrows will be retrieved only after all archers have shot their arrows!

Archery is a fair, healthy and safe sport as long as all athletes adhere to the rules!

Brainteaser page

Here are some brainteasers for you. Have fun figuring them out! You will find the solutions on the solutions page in the back of the book.

1 *Which archer hits the bull's-eye?*

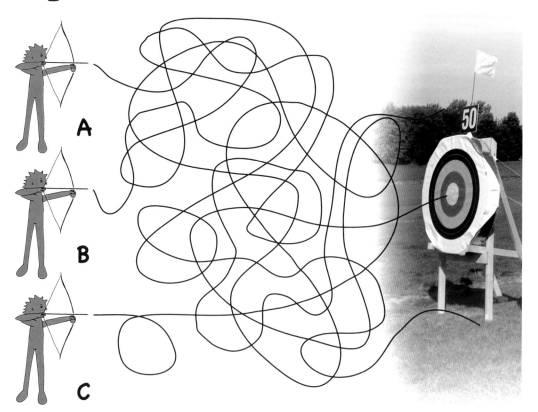

72

2 Who prowled the forest of Nottingham with bow and arrow together with his merry band to rob the rich and give the loot to the poor?

A _____

The famous German poet, Friedrich Schiller, wrote a drama about a father who was forced to shoot an apple from his son's head with bow and arrow as punishment. What is the name of this Swiss folk hero?

B _____

In which movie based on the trilogy by J.R.R. Tolkien does an elven archer named Legolas accompany the hobbit Frodo on his dangerous quest?

C _____

3 *Fill in the missing items! You will then see an important part of the bow in the horizontal row.*

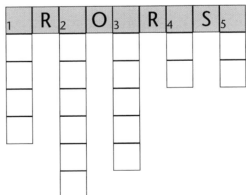

1 Archery projectile
2 Letting go of the bowstring to let the arrow fly
3 A bow is not a toy, but a …
4 End loop of a bowstring
5 Leather or plastic finger protection on drawing hand.

. . . . . . 7 Rifle Shooting

With the invention of firearms, shooting for hunting and shooting in the military have also evolved into shooting as a sport. Shooting sports have been practiced, particularly in shooting clubs, for nearly 100 years in Germany, or even 150 years in the UK. Did you know that most shooting athletes practice rifle shooting?

In this chapter we have compiled the most important facts about rifle shooting for young rifle shooters. You will learn some things about the sports equipment, the shooting range and the clothing. In addition there are the technical elements – firing position aiming and the trigger.

Even the little ones can train with the safe laser light rifle, but the use of air rifles is not recommended for children under the age of 18. But if you are very talented you may be permitted to participate in air rifle competitions at a younger age.

Shooting range

At the shooting range, air powered rifess are fired at targets from a distance of 10 to 25 yards meters. The shooting areas are separated by shooting tables. The rifle and ammunition can be placed on the table. If the shooting range has a cable pull system, you can see your shot pattern right away, because of course you quickly want to know how successful your shot was.

The pros shoot on electronic ranges. There a virtual target can be seen on a monitor. Many shooting ranges offer rifle rests for young shooting athletes. A tripod or a sling (see photo) helps the beginner with steady aiming.

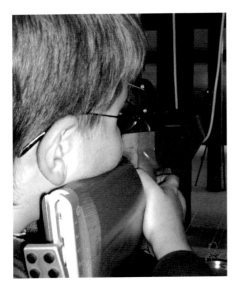

This beak rest is great idea!

Rules on the shooting range

- Shooting on the shooting range may only occur as long as the responsible supervisory staff is present.

- When loading or unloading the rifle, the muzzle must always be pointed towards the target.

- During target practice the muzzle must always be pointed at the target.

- Turning around with a loaded rifle on the range is prohibited.

- Anyone who disrupts the training on the shooting range must leave the area.

Shooting sports are fun, but only if all athletes adhere to the safety rules at the shooting range.

A shooting range for laser light rifles can easily be set up just about anywhere.

Air rifle

What would a rifle shooter be without a rifle? This sporting firearm is a piece of sports equipment, like a ball for a soccer player, a foil for a foil fencer, or a golf club for a golfer. You want to handle it safely and skillfully and definitely hit a "10" as often as possible.

Construction

Of course you want to be totally familiar with your sports equipment and know the names of the different parts.

Stock | Diopter | Barrel | Front sight tunnel | Trigger | Forend | Cartridge | Butt

Junior model air rifles are available for children to train with. They are smaller and lighter than the adult versions.

The air rifle is a great piece of sports equipment that must be handled very carefully by the shooter. Safety rules!

Laser light rifle

A laser light rifle is especially well suited for a beginner. The laser light rifle does not emit a projectile but rather a short pulse of light that hits the receiver target. If you should make a mistake while handling this piece of sports equipment, not much can happen. In addition the shooting range can simply be set up in large well-lit rooms or a gymnasium.

Rifle care

The accuracy of your sports equipment also depends on how dirty the barrel is. That is why the air rifle must occasionally be cleaned. Since you will probably start out shooting with a club-owned rifle, your coach will show you how to clean it. A cleaning cord with felt pellets works best.

Due to their design, laser light rifles don't require special cleaning. It is sufficient to dust off all of the parts or wipe them off with a damp cloth.

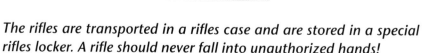

The rifles are transported in a rifles case and are stored in a special rifles locker. A rifle should never fall into unauthorized hands!

Ammunition

Unlike shooters at a carnival who are trying to hit small tubes or plastic flowers, shooting athletes don't shoot with bullets. They use pellets.

A pellet is made of lead and has a 4.5 mm diameter.

Just like the rifles, the ammunition is also stored securely and inaccessibly to unauthorized individuals.

Targets

Athletic competitions require specific targets. The ring numbers and distances must be exact. You can look up the regulations on the National Rifle Association's website at www.nrahq.org.

The black center circle on the target is also called *bull's-eye*.

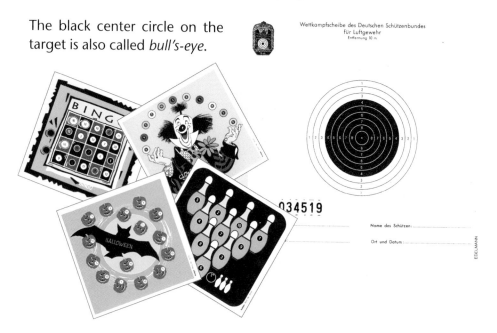

But there are also many different fun and novelty targets for practice shooting, recreational shooting or contests. They are entertaining and the configuration of the target faces differs.

The challenge is always to hit the exact center or to get as close as possible.

Flower meadow

Here we have drawn a fun target. There are twelve flowers for you to pick (hit) in this flower meadow. Make a drawing or a copy of this target for a contest.

- Everyone gets twelve shots. How many flowers did you hit?
- Who needs the fewest shots to "pick" all twelve flowers?

Shooting for fun

Now it's your turn! Design your own novelty target and come up with a funny game rule. You can make a copy or a drawing of the target later and use it at practice.

The rules: _____

_____

Clothing

Of course you won't need special shooting clothing for your initial practice sessions. Wear practical clothing that allows you to move freely.

But surely you are already interested in the special clothing of shooting athletes and its important purpose. That is why we would like to include a brief description.

Shooting jacket

The shooting jacket is made from heavy canvas or leather. It provides support for the upper body, particularly in a standing firing position. Pads minimize the pressure and are slip resistant at the contact points.

Shooting pants

The heavy-duty canvas or leather pants also lend support to the shooter's foothold. Pads on the seat and knees are particularly useful in a kneeling firing position.

Shooting shoes

The shooting shoes have a flat sole that is flexible at the ball of the foot for a secure foothold. The upper material is soft and pliable. The tall shaft provides additional stability for the ankle. Walking in them won't look elegant – but you will have a secure foothold!

Shooting gloves

Regardless of which techniques you use to support your rifle, the glove protects the support hand from the heavy strain it causes. Additional rubber knobs or coatings keep the rifle from slipping.

Head cover and blinder

In the beginning, a well fitting headband is a sufficient head cover. To be able to see the sights with only the aiming eye you cover up the non-aiming eye. For that you can slide a slim piece of cardboard under your headband. Blinking interferes with the aiming process, which is why you should keep both eyes open.

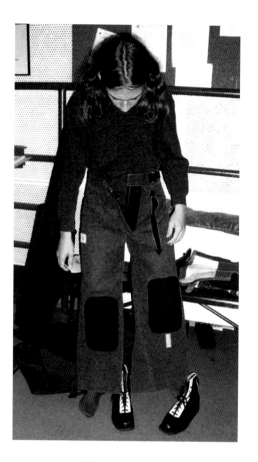

Hearing protection

When live ammunition is being used, every shooter must wear hearing protection. Your hearing is an important but very sensitive organ. That is why it must absolutely be protected from those loud pops – not just at competitions but also at practice! It is how you can protect yourself from future hearing damage.

There are specific rules for competition clothing. You can ask your coach about that.

85

Rifle shooting technique

In rifle shooting there are three firing positions.

- Prone
- Standing
- Kneeling

Your first shooting attempts with the air rifle should be made sitting or lying down with your rifle on a rest. There will be less wobbling and you can focus on the correct sight picture without any problems. Later you will learn to shoot while standing. The most difficult way to shoot is while kneeling.

Prone firing position

Lying down and aiming

In the beginning, you lie down on your stomach with your arms folded without wearing shooting clothing. Align yourself with the target so you feel like you are lying vertically directly behind the target. Make sure you are comfortable, nothing pinches and your clothes give you sufficient freedom of movement. Later, you will be able to feel the work your muscles did in firing position.

Picking up and fitting the rifle

At first the coach places the rifle on the shooting aid (e.g. a knee pad). If you are right-handed he will position your left hand underneath the rifle so the left elbow can be propped up on the pad. With the help of your coach you then fit the rifle into the shoulder pocket as close as possible to the neck. You grasp the pistol grip with your right hand and then also prop the right elbow on the pad.

Positioning the trigger finger

With the wrist as straight as possible, the trigger hand now grasps the pistol grip. The trigger finger is placed gently on the trigger.

Checking the aim

Now the cheek is layed against the stock and you look through the center of the diopter. How does the target image look? Are you at the exact center of the target or do you need to adjust a little?

87

Standing firing position

When you begin with the standing firing position, your coach will help you to adjust the rifle to your physical proportions. This is important because you want to be able to stand still while aiming without contorting yourself.

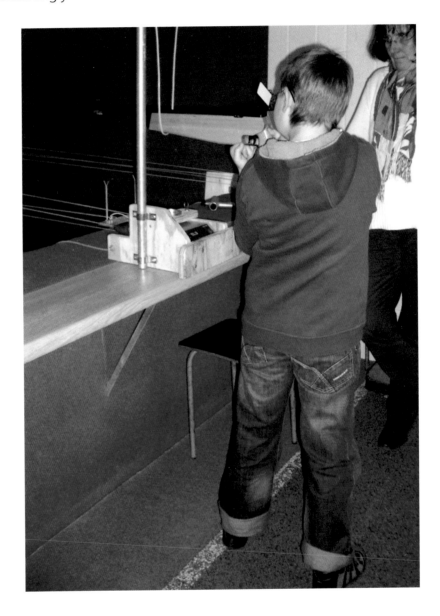

This is how the standing firing position is executed

Here is an illustration of the most important aspects of the standing firing position. Detailed explanations are given on the following pages.

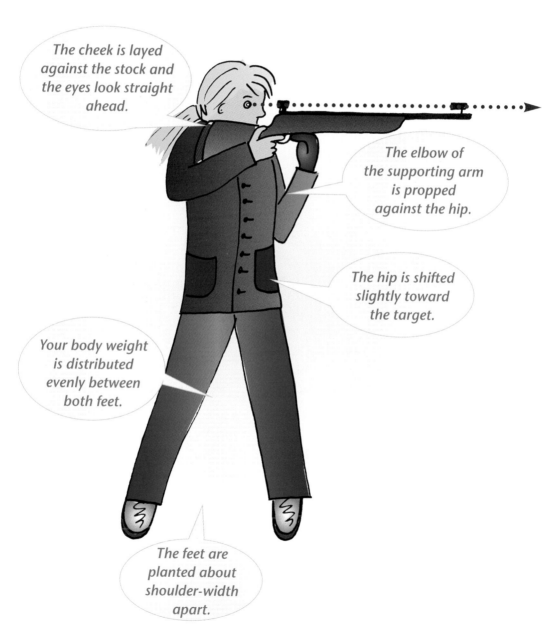

89

This is what you have to pay particular attention to

Foot position

You stand firmly on both feet at a right angle to the target. The feet are parallel and about shoulder-width apart.

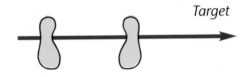

Leg position

The knees are straight but not hyper-extended. They cannot be rigid.

Hip

The hip is shifted forward slightly, towards the target. Always make sure that it is not twisted. The hip is always parallel to the firing line.

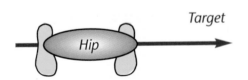

Upper body

The upper body leans back slightly. The shoulders are not pulled up and remain relaxed. This also keeps the back muscles from tightening up.

Support arm

The elbow of the support hand is propped against the hip. Find the right position for the elbow so you can support the rifle without using additional muscle power.

Trigger hand

The trigger arm is held high enough to allow the stock to rest securely against the shoulder. The wrist on the trigger hand is straight. The rifle is held firmly, but not clenched, at the pistol grip.

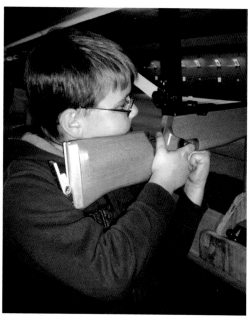

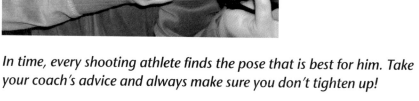

Head position

By resting the head, you complete the balanced equilibrium. With your head as upright as possible, lay your cheek against the cheek piece. The rifle moves toward the head.

In time, every shooting athlete finds the pose that is best for him. Take your coach's advice and always make sure you don't tighten up!

Aiming

When you aim the eye, diopter, sight, and target point are aligned. That sounds easy at first, but it requires lots of concentration and of course practice.

The coach has various aids for you so you can start by just concentrating on aiming. You practice in prone position or sitting and the rifle barrel is placed in a sling or on a rifle rest. He will also make aiming easier for you with the choice of target. After all, you want to succeed!

Aiming technique

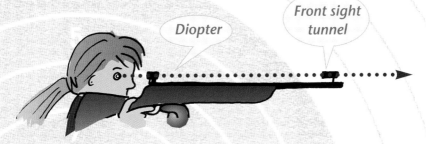

Diopter

Front sight tunnel

The rifle has an aiming device for precision aiming. This includes the diopter and the front sight tunnel with aperture. There are different sizes and types of apertures. The shooter has to try them out and talk to the coach to figure out which is the best one for her. Beginners often also practice without an aperture.

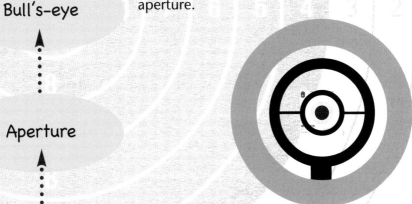

Bull's-eye

Aperture

Diopter

Eye

When you aim, you look through the exact middle of the diopter. There you will see the aperture in the center and in it's center the bull's eye. This concentric view gives you a precise target image.

For a good shot the aiming process should not take more than eight seconds!

Mistakes you must avoid!

Look at how the little mistake guys practice rifle shooting. What are they doing wrong?

1

2

Don't be surprised that these little guys are making such big mistakes! But we had to exaggerate a little to make the mistakes more recognizable. You will find the solutions to the mistakes in the solutions chapter.

In these photos you can see Julie deliberately making mistakes while shooting the rifle.

Can you see them?

Exercises

Strong back and abdominal muscles are particularly important for having a firm stance. You also need strength so you can soon hold your sports equipment steady without help. Here we have compiled a few exercises for you.

Strong back

Lie on your back and raise your pelvis. Chest, stomach, thighs and knees form a straight line. (2 x 20 seconds).

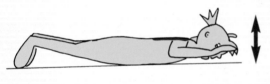

Lie flat on your stomach, bend your elbows and raise your arms and head slightly off the floor. Keep your eyes on the floor. (3 x 10 seconds).

Hold a ball with your arms extended forward. Arms and legs lift slightly off the floor. (3 x 10 seconds). Squeeze your legs together at the same time.

Hold the ball above your bottom. Pass it from hand to hand (3 x 10 repetitions).

Stand with your knees slightly bent, feet shoulder-width apart, and extend your arms overhead. Now bend forward while keeping your back straight.

Strong abdominals

Whenever someone strengthens the back muscles he should not forget to strengthen the abdominal muscles (antagonists) as well. These muscle groups (back and abdominal muscles) must be worked in a way that keeps them balanced!

Lie on your back with your knees bent. Your back is firmly on the floor. Now try slightly raising your upper body.

Now rest your legs on a stool or a chair (3 x 20 repetitions each).

Bring your right elbow to your left knee and then your left elbow to your right knee. Now you are also working the **oblique abdominal muscles**.

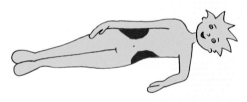

You can also strengthen them by lying on your side and propping yourself up on your forearm. Now push your upper body up until your body is in a straight line.

Strong arms

You can only hold the sports equipment steady if you are strong enough. Someone who is weak will wobble. It would be great if your parents could help you construct a fake rifle. It should have the approximate shape, length (3.5 feet) and weight (approx. 16 lbs) of an air rifle. It could be a board, a fence slat, or a plastic tube filled with sand. Then you can practice aiming, and especially holding and supporting the rifle at home.

Always switch sides to avoid one-sided strain!

You can find many more exercises on the yellow practice pages in this book!

Safety first!

There are important rules to make sure that practice is fun and you can feel good and safe while training. Everyone must observe them, and everyone must also make sure that other children and adults adhere to them.

- Only an authorized adult with a weapon's license has a key to the firearms locker.
- The coach lays out the firearms at the shooting range and gives specific commands.
- The firearms locker always remains locked.
- The ammunition is always stored safely and separate from the firearms.
- Children are permitted at the shooting range only when a shooting range attendant (trained licensed adult) is present.
- Everyone keeps the shooting range orderly and helps to clean up.

Only when the coach is sure that you have mastered all safety regulations will he let you shoot with ammunition!

Hey Sammy, are you going to shooting practice again? Wouldn't you like to just fire a few rounds first?

My rifle is a piece of sports equipment and I will only unpack it at the shooting range. I think you've seen too many westerns!

Important rules at the shooting range

◉ Handle your sports equipment with care. Keep your rifle clean and make sure it is always stored securely.

◉ Check your rifle before every use!

◉ Shoot only when an attendant is present at the shooting range.

◉ Do not go to the shooting range while under stress! All negative thoughts like rage, anger or irritation must be blanked out when shooting. Relax and concentrate!

◉ Focus completely on your target before you begin to shoot!

◉ Concentrate on each shot anew! You always want to fire a clean shot. That's why your trigger finger only curls when your intuition tells you: "Now!"

◉ Put your rifle down if you are feeling unsure, anxious or disturbed. Then start the aiming process over again!

◉ Don't let anything distract you during the final phase of shooting preparation! You focus only on the target image and the trigger finger.

◉ Move only the trigger finger when you fire, not the entire hand or even body!

◉ Don't forget to follow-through for a few seconds after you fire!

◉ _____

◉ _____

◉ _____

You can use the blank lines to write down tips and suggestions from your coach or experienced shooting athletes!

······ 8 Pistol Shooting

Most shooting athletes start out with the rifle because this discipline is often more widely practiced and holds a longer tradition in shooting sports. But the pistol also has great advantages as you saw in the interview with Ralf Schumann. Anyone who has tried pistol shooting is usually very excited about this interesting discipline.

The great challenge of an air pistol

⊙ Unlike the rifle and the bow, the pistol is operated with just one hand. That is why the shooter must have a lot of strength in the arm holding the gun and a steady aim so he doesn't wobble when he pulls the trigger.

⊙ Because the pistol has a short barrel, it also has a short sight line. Small mistakes made while aiming have a particularly negative effect on the shooting result.

Rifle shooters should also occasionally shoot a pistol as a way to improve their shooting performance.

Air pistol

There is hardly an action film that doesn't have a gun in it. There is lots of loud banging around, auto tires are shot out, and even people are threatened. But all of that has nothing to do with your sports equipment. You have an air pistol with which you, calmly and with concentration, want to hit the "10".

Construction

The air pistol operates with compressed air. The compressed air is located in the cartridge underneath the barrel. You can fire many shots with it before it has to be refilled. The indicator at the front lets you know when the cartridge is empty.

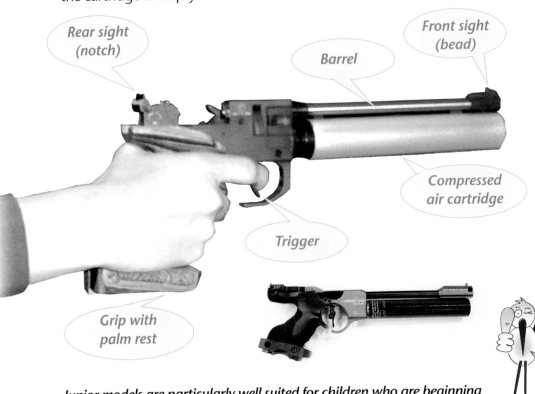

Rear sight (notch)

Barrel

Front sight (bead)

Compressed air cartridge

Trigger

Grip with palm rest

Junior models are particularly well suited for children who are beginning shooters. These are lighter and smaller than pistols for adults.

Laser light pistol

Before you begin using an air pistol you can also start with laser light shooting. These ranges can be set up anywhere and are easy to operate. It is a way for you to practice without the popping noises or fear of that first shot. Ask your coach about it!

If your club does not have a laser light set-up, your coach will gradually guide you towards that first shot with some preliminary exercises.

Pistol care

Always handle your pistol with care! You can only shoot successfully with it if you take good care of it! The barrel of the pistol should be cleaned periodically. Since you will likely start out with a club-owned pistol, your coach will show you how to clean it.

The pistols are transported in a pistol case and are stored in a pistol locker! A pistol should never fall into unauthorized hands!

Due to their design, laser light pistols don't require special cleaning. It is sufficient to dust off all of the parts or wipe them off with a damp cloth.

Ammunition

Like the rifle shooters, pistol shooters also use pellets. Because of their special shape, their target entry is cleaner than bullets.

A pellet is made of lead and has a 4.5 mm diameter. It is inserted into the barrel with the smooth side to the front. As with the air rifle, only a single shot is loaded.

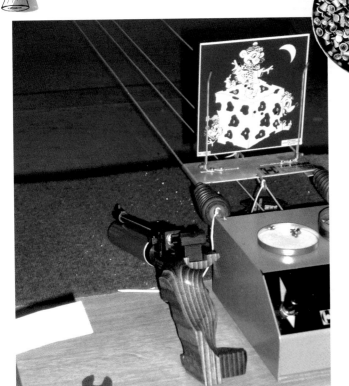

Just like the pistols, the ammunition is also always stored securely and inaccessibly to unauthorized individuals.

If a specific number of shots per series is specified, put the exact number of pellets in the top of the ammo box. Now you can keep track.

Targets

Athletic competitions require specific targets. The ring numbers and distances must be exact. You can look up the regulations on the National Rifle Association's website at *www.nrahq.org*.

The black center circle on the target is also called **bull's-eye**.

The air pistol target is bigger than the rifle target. For a 10 m distance it has a 155.5 mm diameter for the outer ring.

But there are also many different fun and novelty targets for practice shooting, recreational shooting or contests. They are entertaining and the configuration of the target faces differs.

Of course the challenge is always to hit the exact center or to get as close as possible.

Clothing and accessories

Unlike rifle shooters, pistol shooters are not permitted to wear special clothing to support the body. Nevertheless, for pistol shooting it is also important that you wear appropriate athletic clothing that ...

- doesn't restrict your freedom of movement or hinder you.
- will ventilate you when it's hot and protect you from intense sun light.
- will protect you from the cold so you don't cool down while shooting.

Pistol shooting is your sport – so dress like it!

Shirt and pants

Manufacturers offer special functional clothing for top shooters. But in the beginning, a regular tracksuit or other comfortable athletic clothes are just fine.

Sleeveless vests and long underwear can help keep your muscles warm in cold indoor ranges and open shooting stands. Then you can work properly and really feel everything.

Shooting shoes

For a firm stance you should wear shoes with flat even soles. Slightly forward-sloping cushioning also improves the foothold. Official competition rules specify that shoes must not extend above the ankle.

Head cover

Bright interior lights or intense sunlight change the size of your pupils and that affects your target image. It makes precise aiming difficult and the eyes quickly get tired. That's why you should definitely wear a hat with a brim or a sun visor. Always wear this sun protection during practice so you can get used to it.

Blinder and shooting glasses

Both eyes remain open while aiming, but most shooters cover the non-aiming eye. In the beginning, simply slide a strip of cardboard under an elastic band, headband, or a cap. Later on, there are special shooting glasses with a solid nosepiece, blinders and lenses. This is particularly useful for people who wear glasses.

Hearing protection

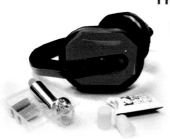

It can get very noisy on a shooting range. Our hearing is very sensitive and should always (practice and competition) be protected from those popping noises. This also applies to compressed air disciplines. Protective earmuffs or earplugs are well suited for hearing protection.

Pocket hand warmers

Shooting ranges can be cold and uncomfortable. Fingers quickly get cold and stiff. Accurate firing becomes difficult. A little pocket hand warmer is inexpensive and quickly warms your fingers!

Pistol Shooting Technique

Firing position procedure

The arm holding the gun is fully extended and is a direct extension of the barrel axis.

The head is erect and turned towards the target.

The upper body is erect and both shoulders stay down.

You body weight is distributed equally between both feet.

The hip is not cocked or twisted.

The feet are parallel and about shoulder-width apart.

Setting up at the shooting range

A very important prerequisite for practice and competition is the correct set-up at the shooting range. For shooting athletes this means accurately lining up the firing position with the target.

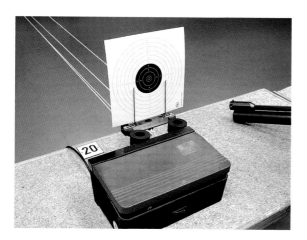

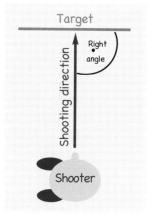

• *First you insert a target and move it to the aim point.*

Setting up on 10m-ranges with a cable pull system is relatively easy. To find the center of the target you can orientate yourself by the cables. But watch out:

• *Not all systems are mounted at a right angle to the target.*
• *At competitions electronic systems are often used for shooting. That means no cables, no auxiliary lines, and no paper targets.*

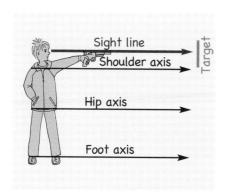

Even without auxiliary lines, try to immediately position yourself vertically to the target at its center.

• *If you are a right-handed shooter your right hip must point directly at the target.*
• *Your foot axis and your hip axis remain exactly parallel to your shoulder axis and your sight line.*

109

This is what you must pay attention to in firing position

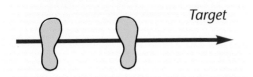

Target

Foot position

Stand firmly on both feet at a right angle to the target. The feet are parallel and about shoulder-width apart. Your weight is evenly distributed between both feet.

Can't figure out the correct foot distance? Here's a tip from Sammy! 1- 2- 3!

1. Stand with your feet together at a right angle to the target!
2. Now turn your toes out as far as you can.
3. Now your feet should be about hip-width apart.

 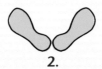

1.   2.   3.

Do you now stand as directed? If you are still wobbling forward or backward, move your feet a little farther apart and turn your toes in slightly more!

Leg position

Keeping your legs straight is very important for a firm stance. But you should not hyperextend your legs in firing position. You are only able to balance yourself at any time and feel exactly where you are and which muscles are working, if your kneecaps are relaxed while standing.

Later, after you have practiced enough, you can skip the 3-point method for correct foot placement and immediately assume your own foot and leg position.

Posture

The upper body is erect and straight. The hip is not cocked or twisted. Your body weight is equally distributed between both legs and your center of gravity is in the middle.

Shooting arm

The shooting arm is extended. Shoulder, elbow and wrist are steady. Make sure you don't pull the shoulder up as you lift the arm.

Non-shooting arm

The non-shooting arm hangs loosely at the side and the shoulder is also relaxed. You are even looser if you rest your hand in your belt or waistband. Or just put it in your jacket pocket.

Head position

Hold your head erect and straight. When you turn toward the target, the muscles in your neck and cervical spine should not tighten up.

Are you having trouble with the loose turning of the head? Exercises that require turning your head to the side are always helpful. But be careful: Don't overdo it!

111

Fitting the sporting firearm

Once you have set up the correct position on your stand you can pick up your pistol and properly fit it in your hand.

Here is the sequence:

- *As a right-hander you pick up the sporting firearm with your left hand and place it in the right hand.*

  - *It is inserted into the valley between the index finger and thumb.*

  - *The hand holds the grip so that the forearm forms an extension of the sight line.*

- *The first phalanx of the index finger is placed in the exact center of the trigger.*

  - *When holding the pistol, the valley between thumb and index finger bears the bulk of the weight.*

  - *Your thumb rests on the thumb rest without putting pressure on it.*

Holding the sporting firearm correctly won't always be easy. As your body changes your hand and fingers will also grow. The grip on a club-owned sporting firearm won't always fit your hand perfectly. Once you are an experienced shooter you may own a sporting firearm with a customized grip.

Aiming

In the beginning, you just want to keep hitting the target and later, the bull's-eye. To do so you must learn to aim at the center of the target and then curl the trigger finger at just the right moment. A good shooting technique, a trained eye, and of course the sighting device on your sporting firearm are very helpful.

Sighting device

The sighting device on the pistol helps you with aiming. They are the rear and front sights (notch and bead). To learn the aiming sequence you often practice with the pistol resting on a support – first sitting and then standing.

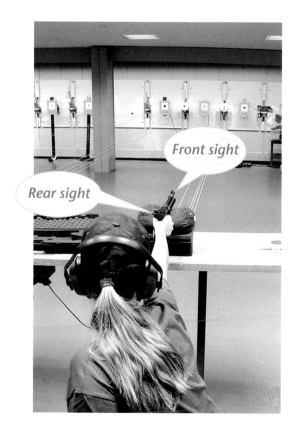

Front sight

Rear sight

A shooter's kneepad or a pillow is a perfect support for the pistol. Now you can practice on the actual target image without too much physical effort.

From the start sit in the correct position to achieve a straight sight line with the upper body!

Target image

What should the image look like when you aim? Here is an illustration and a description for you.

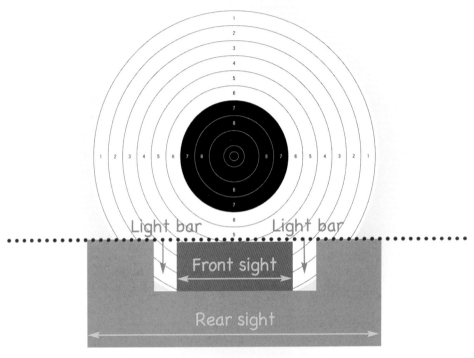

- The adjustment of **rear and front sights** is called **sight alignment**. It means that the sights are adjusted so the front sight is in the center of the rear sight and the edges are lined up.

- The **light bars** are of equal width.

- The distance from the upper edge of the front sight to the aiming mark is approximately two white rings.

Beginners also start practicing with the target image on a white target without an aim mark. Then you only have to focus on the light bars.

Aiming process

In the beginning you won't often get the correct target image freehand. The arm gets tired quickly and that makes it hard to cleanly focus on all of the distances and lines. Inexperienced shooters keep looking back and forth between rear sight, front sight and aim mark. In doing so you quickly lose control over the sighting device and the sporting firearm becomes canted. The shot goes who-knows-where, but not at the center of the target.

That's why you start by shooting at white targets without the black aim mark. Then you only have to pay attention to the light bars and focus the front sight with your eye. You'll see that you can already shoot a group like this!

If you can manage the target image with sight alignment without an aim mark, you can switch to a target with aim mark. In addition to the light bars you now also have to pay attention to the two white circles.

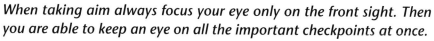

When taking aim always focus your eye only on the front sight. Then you are able to keep an eye on all the important checkpoints at once.

115

Firing

When firing the gun the trick is to move the trigger finger independently from the rest of the hand.

- *The trigger finger is not in contact with anything.*
- *The trigger finger only touches the trigger with the first phalanx (finger pad).*
- *The trigger is gently pulled straight back so the pistol isn't pushed out of the sight line.*

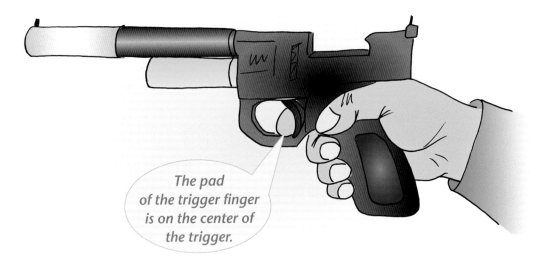

The pad of the trigger finger is on the center of the trigger.

Pressure point

The **trigger weight** of an air pistol is 500 grams and it is shot with a pressure point trigger. The **pressure point** is a small resistor that you can feel and must push past during trigger travel until the discharge. The way to the pressure point is called pre-pull.

If you have a very small hand and short fingers it is possible that your index finger won't reach far enough around the trigger. In that case your coach can move the trigger farther back or remove some wood from the grip.

Motion sequence

1 Preparation phase
- *Set up relative to the target and establish the firing position. Load the firearm.*
- *Practice firing position with eyes closed and open. Check firearm and sights.*
- *Check posture.*
- *Fine tune aim at bull's-eye.*

2 Starting phase
- *Lift firearm to the upper edge of target with extended arm.*
- *Calm breathing raises the chest and supports the lifting of the arm.*
- *Start sighting in and check trigger finger.*

3 Work phase
- *Slowly lower arm until sights are just below aim mark.*
- *The air slowly leaves the lungs.*
- *Pull trigger up to pressure point.*

4 Trigger phase
- *Once the target image has been reached, the pressure on the trigger increases.*
- *The shot is discharged.*

5 Follow-though and return phase
- *When the shot discharges, try to "see through the shot."*
- *Continue to hold your firearm for a moment and visualize where the shot went.*

Sometimes you may be disturbed while you are aiming, you can't concentrate, or your strength is fading. If you are not able to go through the motion sequence until the end, stop and start over with the starting phase.

117

Mistakes you must avoid!

Look at how the little blue mistake guys practice pistol shooting. What are they doing wrong?

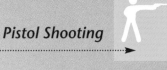

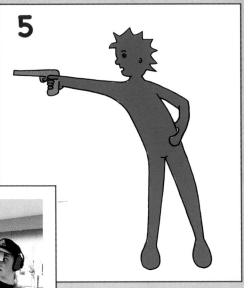

Don't be surprised that these little guys and Julie are making such big mistakes! But we had to exaggerate a little to make the mistakes more recognizable. You will find the solutions to the mistakes in the solutions chapter.

Strength exercises

To be able to hold the sporting firearm steady you need sufficient strength in the shoulders, arms and hands. Here are a few exercises you can also do at home, outside of your regular training sessions.

Strengthening the shoulder muscles

- *Hold the ends of the band tightly in your hands.*

- *Put your right foot on the band.*

- *Turn your head to the right and pull the band up with the right arm until it is horizontal.*

- *Briefly hold this position and then slowly lower the arm.*

- *Now switch sides!*

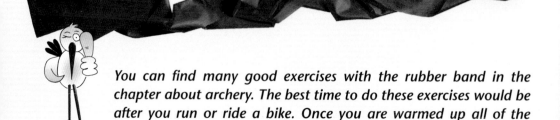

You can find many good exercises with the rubber band in the chapter about archery. The best time to do these exercises would be after you run or ride a bike. Once you are warmed up all of the muscles are well prepared.

Strengthening arms and shoulders

Date	Seconds/ repetitions

Find on object you can easily span with your hand. A water bottle is best. (If the bottle is too heavy, drink some of the water!)

- Hold the bottle with your arm extended, and count how many seconds you are able to hold it like this.
- Lift the bottle, – "Bang"! – Lower it! After ten repetitions take a short break.
- Make a small chart (like this one) and record your results every day!
- Are you getting better? Have a contest with friends and siblings.

Strong hands and fingers

Hold a rubber ring or a hard rubber ball in your hand and squeeze hard.

- Hold the squeeze for a while.
- At the same time, extend the arm as you would to shoot a pistol.

Always remember: Never train one-sided, just strengthening the same arm and the same hand! In order to have balanced muscles you must also do all of the exercises with the opposite side.

Quiz for shooting athletes

We have listed four possible answers to each question. But only one of the four answers is correct. Can you find it?

1 *Which of these sports does not require aiming?*

A   Bowling   B   Golf

C   Darts   D   Bingo

2 *What do you call a shot that doesn't hit the desired target?*

A   Ticket   B   Slip

C   Error   D   Miss

3 *Which profession does not use loaded firearms?*

A   Pop stars   B   Hunters

C   Police   D   Soldiers

4 *What do you call the release of a shot?*

A   Blasting away   B   Banging

C   Firing   D   Popping

You will find the correct answers in the solutions pages!

5 *What do you call the basic body position while shooting?*

A   Spread position   B   Firing position

C   Cover position   D   Stance

6 *How are sport shooting firearms transported?*

A   In a case   B   In a backpack

C   In a handbag   D   In a neck pouch

7 *What is the name of the most successful German shooting athlete?*

A   Maik Eckhard   B   Ralf Schumacher

C   Ralf Schumann   D   Michael Schumacher

8 *What does a shooting athlete aim for?*

A   Goal   B   Basket

C   Hole   D   Target

Help, I'm lost!

Imagine this: Sammy's last competition was out-of-town at an unfamiliar shooting stand. He wanted to make a quick trip to the men's room. But then he couldn't find his way back to the stand. Can you figure out which way he needed to go?

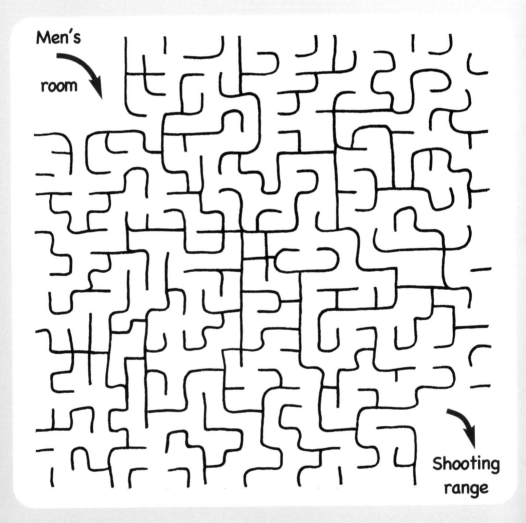

Men's
room

Shooting
range

. . . . 9 Fit and Healthy

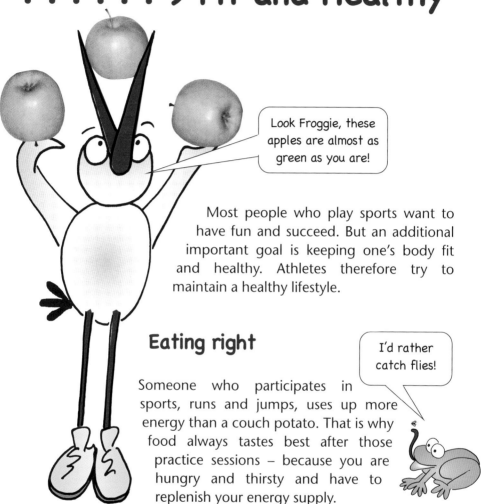

> Look Froggie, these apples are almost as green as you are!

Most people who play sports want to have fun and succeed. But an additional important goal is keeping one's body fit and healthy. Athletes therefore try to maintain a healthy lifestyle.

Eating right

> I'd rather catch flies!

Someone who participates in sports, runs and jumps, uses up more energy than a couch potato. That is why food always tastes best after those practice sessions – because you are hungry and thirsty and have to replenish your energy supply.

Almost all children like to eat chocolate, chips, French fries and pizza. But that's not the best food for athletes, particularly if you eat these things too frequently and in large quantities. These foods contain too much fat.

The better meal for an athlete consists of whole grain bread with cheese, pasta, fruit and yoghurt. There are many foods that are healthy and taste good, too. Try to have a varied and moderate diet.

125

This athlete is really hungry after practice. He would like to just eat and drink everything at once. What would you recommend? Cross out anything that in your opinion is not very healthy!

Which food should you eat more frequently during the day, and when you need a snack? Cross out every L, Y, M, A, X, E, K and D

F	D	K	A	R	E	X	Y	M	L	A
M	E	L	M	A	U	D	I	K	D	Y
Y	A	D	D	L	K	Y	M	A	M	T

If you sweat you have to drink regularly

When you sweat during training and while playing, your gym clothes are often soaked and you can see beads of perspiration on your skin. Sweating isn't bad – in fact, it's very healthy. But your body misses the fluids you lose when you sweat. That's when you have to drink a lot so your body once again has enough fluids.

Your trainer, coach or teacher will plan water breaks when you have been sweating.

Thirst quenchers

Pure juice and soft drinks are not suitable for replenishing fluids.
They contain too much sugar.

The best thirst quenchers are:

* Water, uncarbonated mineral water
* Water and juice mix (apple, orange or cherry juice mixed with water)
* Herbal tea or fruit tea (also sweetened with honey)

When you are thirsty and drink, you have to be careful not to drink too hastily. It is better to take smaller sips more often. Be careful not to fill your stomach so full that you will barely be able to move.

Don't choose drinks that are really cold or your body has to expend additional energy to warm up that fluid and get it up to body temperature!

127

Don't forget to warm up!

Surely your coach always does a warm-up at the beginning of a training session.

It is important that your muscles become warm, loose and flexible through different exercises. That is how you protect yourself from injuries.

To warm up you can jog or do some easy jumping exercises.

Swing your arms or move them in circles.

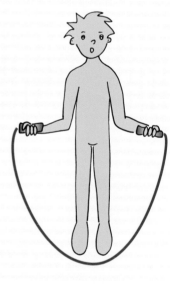

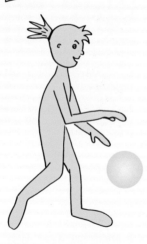

Dribble the ball at a walk and at a run. As you dribble, jump, spin around and clap your hands.

Even when you do exercises at home or play with your friends – don't forget to warm up!

128

Holding the ball overhead, stretch yourself really long and stand on your toes – like you are trying to lay the ball in the basket.

Now bend over with straight legs and set the ball down.

Put your hands on your hips and keeping your upper body straight, rotate your torso to the left and to the right.

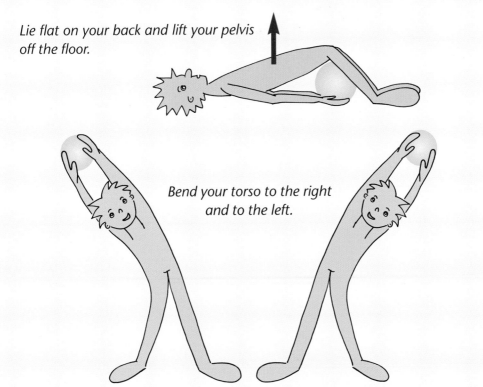

Lie flat on your back and lift your pelvis off the floor.

Bend your torso to the right and to the left.

129

. . . . . . 10 Joining a Club

You can throw at cans or play darts at home, in the back yard, or at the fair. But anyone who wants to practice a real shooting sport needs to join a club. Experienced trainers and coaches will show you how to safely handle the equipment. The equipment is checked regularly and the shooting range is safe.

There you belong to a team and can participate in actual competitions.

How to find a club

⊙ If your parents give their consent, look for a shooting organization or a gun club in your area.

⊙ If you are lucky, family members, friends, or classmates are already members in a club and will bring you along to a practice.

⊙ Most shooting organizations have bulletin boards, displays, or websites. That's where phone numbers or practice times are listed.

⊙ Make an appointment for a try out. Take the time to see how everything works. You will meet the coaches and other children; you'll see how the training is done and how the safety rules are adhered to. Of course everything will be new and unfamiliar at first. That's normal!

⊙ If you like it and the coach says you are suited for shooting sports, then you should sign up. You will become a club member and receive a membership card.

131

My first shooting sports organization

Here I am learning to shoot:

_____

_____

My first day was on:

_____

My trainers are:

_____

You can paste photos of your friends here!

My friends and teammates

You can collect signatures from all of your friends in your practice group on this page!

Competition results

Writing down competition results is interesting and fun.

You can record them on this page.

Competition/Date	Results

Competition/Date	Results

Making sure everyone is having fun

First we want to tell you about a strange practice group. Do you see what's going on here?

What is going on here?

The coach has already begun with the warm-up when Tina runs in with her boots on to get the key to the locker room. Tom can't jump properly because he is finishing his apple, Lisa and Julie are having a noisy chat, Kyle is crying because his jeans are too tight to stretch in, and Anne slipped in the apple juice that Tania spilled…

Do you think that practicing with this group is fun? Surely not! Well, to be honest, we made this story up. Nowhere is it that bad! Or is there a little bit of truth to this after all?

Rules are necessary

To make sure all children have fun practicing and are able to learn there are training rules. They are specified by the trainer or coach and discussed as a group.

All of the athletes make sure that the rules are obeyed. Then everyone can have fun at practice.

Important rules

Here is a list of rules we think are very important for the group and at the shooting stand or the archery range.

- ☺ Always arrive to practice on time! You miss too much if you dawdle!

- ☺ Call if you are sick. When you have an unexcused absence, no one will know if you will be back or will be able to participate in a competition.

- ☺ Don't talk during instructions and exercises or you won't understand everything and will make mistakes.

- ☺ Wear practical athletic clothes.

- ☺ Do not enter the gym with street shoes.

- ☺ The shooting range is not a playground!

- ☺ Playing and goofing off is done away from the shooting range.

- ☺ No chewing gum during practice! But have a drinking bottle handy at the stand or on the archery range.

- ☺ Help each other and be considerate of each other!

☺ _____

☺ _____

☺ _____

☺ _____

☺ _____

What other rules do you have? Add them on the blank lines!

137

F	I	S	H
D	O	C	K

1

How did the FISH get on the DOCK? You can only change one letter in each row!

2

Are these drawings of Sammy and the little frog identical? Not quite! Find twelve differences!

138

. . . . 11 Solutions

Pg. 26

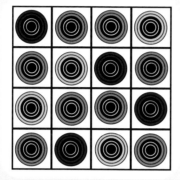

Pg. 36   Thrower **C** scores.

Pg. 64/65   Mistakes in archery

1 The shooter doesn't have his feet shoulder-width apart and therefore has no firm stance in the basic position.
2 The shooter isn't looking at the target during preparation.
3 The shooter isn't standing sideways.
4 The thumb isn't on the thumb rest of the tap.
5 Here the shooter is leaning in the shooting direction. But his back should be taut and he should stand erect.
6 After firing the shooter must follow through and remain in firing position until the arrow hits the target.

Pg. 72   **1** Shooter A hits the bull's-eye.

Pg. 73   **2** A Robin Hood
              B William Tell
              C Lord of the Rings

Pg. 73

A	R	R	O	W	R	E	S	T
R		E		E		Y		A
R		L		A		E		P
O		E		P				
W		A		O				
		S		N				
		E						

Pg. 94/95   **Mistakes in rifle shooting**

1 The shooter has an incorrect foot position and the body is hunched forward.

2 The body faces the target and the support elbow rests on the stomach. This makes the rifle move during breathing.

3 The stock isn't nestled snugly "into the shoulder" but rather sits on the upper arm.

4 The shoulder is pulled up and the posture is tense.

5 The wrist of the trigger hand is bent. This makes a clean pull of the trigger impossible.

Pg. 118/119 **Mistakes in pistol shooting**

1 The pistol is held with both hands.

2 The shooting arm is not extended.

3 The eyes are not on the target.

4 The shoulder is too high and the head is tilted.

5 The body leans forward in direction of the target.

6 The feet are too close together.

7 Feet and body are facing the target instead of being oriented sideways.

Pg. 122/123   Shooting Sports Quiz

1	D	**5**	B
2	D	**6**	A
3	A	**7**	C
4	C	**8**	D

Pg. 124

F	D	K	A	**R**	E	X	Y	M	L	A
M	E	L	M	A	**U**	D	**I**	K	D	Y
Y	A	D	D	L	K	Y	M	A	M	**T**

Pg. 138

F	I	S	H
D	I	S	H
D	I	S	K
D	E	S	K
D	E	C	K
D	O	C	K

141

Here you can design a funny or interesting target! Later on you can make a copy of your design or draw it onto a target of the appropriate size for your discipline. Also list the rules!

. . . . 12 Let's Talk!

If this were a book for adults, these pages for the parents and trainers would of course appear at the very front of the book as the preface. But since it is a book for children we are putting this chapter at the end, sort of as an addendum.

Our beginning shooting athletes are mostly elementary school students who have not yet had very much exposure to books. They are absolutely in need of support from "big people" who can help them with the approach to the book.

The best way to start is by leafing through the book, looking at the pictures and filling in and recording information. This book does not have to be read front to back, but can also be used as a reference work and a personal shooting sports diary.

We chose to combine the three most common shooting sport disciplines in one comprehensive book because the individual disciplines do have many similarities. Every athlete within the larger family of shooting athletes should also be interested in the other disciplines!

Have fun reading together!

143

Dear Parents,

Surely the "alarm bells" went off when your child came home and announced that he wanted to join a shooting organization. All too present are the terrible shooting incidents that have occurred in schools and that most certainly cause you to worry about a recurrence at any time. Shooting equipment is, without a doubt, dangerous and should only be in qualified hands.

Knives, for instance, are also dangerous objects, and every year there are many incidents nationwide that involve their violent misuse. But is that a reason to ban all knives from the kitchen? Of course not! But here, too, rules for their safe handling must be adhered to!

Being cautious and thoughtful when it comes to your child is wise, and that is good! As a responsible parent you should inform yourself about the organization on site and get a close look at everything. Talk to the individuals in charge so you can ultimately make an impartial decision for or against shooting sports together with your child.

But why shooting sports?

As you take a closer look at this little tutorial you will see that shooting is a sport that is linked to an integrated education concept. Being involved in the community of an organization, learning to be dependable, responsible and disciplined in the handling of sports equipment, learning to win and to lose, experiencing personal limitations, motivation, endurance and perseverance in the pursuit of goals, are all part of the formulated educational goals. In addition there is the ability to concentrate and physical control, as well as developing an awareness of physical health combined with the desire for physical fitness and sport appropriate nutrition.

The focus of a research project at the University of Munich, Germany, was to determine whether the concern that the early contact with "weapons" at a shooting organization increases the disposition toward violence in children between the ages of eight and eleven, is justified. The results showed that there was no evidence of differences between "shooting children" and "non-shooting children" in the forming of sensitivity to violence. Simply put: "shooting children" are just normal children!

On the contrary, shooting sports contribute to a decrease in the disposition toward violence, as was largely suspected. A person with a well-defined sense of self does not require scapegoats and escape routes. He recognizes problems and is able to solve them as is appropriate for the situation or individual. His reactions are emotionally suitable. With "Learning Shooting Sports" we would like to demonstrate that this can be learned in a well-balanced manner, and also offer the child support while doing so. A child that is able to build his/her life on this foundation has no reason to seek refuge in irrational coping strategies like addiction or violence. He/She learns to take responsibility for him-/herself and his/her natural and social environment. The book title "Learning Shooting Sports" is part of the program.

One thing we can do together is to continue to improve child-appropriate training and organizational activity. Our book series is meant to contribute to this.

Sports equipment for the little ones

No later than elementary school age do most children look for a recreational activity. They want to learn something interesting outside of school, make new friends and compete against each other. Aiming and scoring – that's fun and very appealing!

But that doesn't mean that even the youngest children can't have fun in a shooting sports organization. Laser light ranges are very safe and the children can practice aiming, shooting and scoring with many different target games and devices, and thus getting prepared for shooting with real equipment in the future.

Be helpful, but with prudence!

Do not let your expectations for your child get too high! What matters most is the enjoyment of the sport and aiming. Excessive ambition would only be harmful. Don't compare your child to others of the same age, because biological development, particularly at this age, can vary greatly. Just focus on your own child and praise his or her progress. Your child will thank you.

Oh no! I promise I'll never miss again!

146

Support from parents

Parental support is in demand in shooting sports, too. Be it for the organization of training attire, rides to practices or chaperoning at

competitions. Some parents or grandparents even get certified as shooting range attendants to help out at the range.

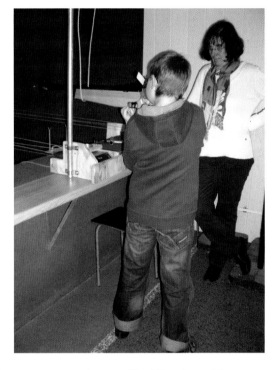

When your child is participating in competitions, some of your family weekends will be affected by the competition schedule. But what could be better than seeing your eager little shooting athlete jump for joy because of a great shot pattern. Or, how much trust and intimacy do parents and children share when some comfort is needed because of a bad competition or loss.

Be glad that your child is getting some regular exercise. Regardless of whether your child will become a successful international super-marksman some day or "just" enjoys his shooting sport and its sense of community.

And one more thing:

Savor the competition and enjoy your child's ability to concentrate, his/her continuously improving technique and athletic ambition. Cheer the children on and be happy about their successful actions. However, parents who shout technical suggestions irritate the children. The children need to make their own decisions, and technical suggestions are the trainer's responsibility.

What a children's shooting sports trainer should have:

Dear Trainer, Dear Coach,

Surely you'll agree that it is a great feeling to see these little guys with their excited faces and expectant eyes. Now it is up to you to introduce them to the shooting sport disciplines.

But all children are different. There are the tall ones and the short ones, self-confident ones and the timid ones, the diligent and the not so diligent, the talented and the less talented. Each child has his/her own little personality with individual qualifications and his/her own developmental history, with hopes and desires, with feelings and needs. They all have our regard in equal measure. Children want to be active, to move and have fun. Particularly in a group they are able to match themselves with their peers and spur each other on.

The most important role model for young shooting athletes is their coach, teacher, or trainer. They watch everything very closely: How he talks to them, how he handles the sports equipment and executes the movements. They also pay close attention to how well their trainer adheres to the rules and safety regulations.

The young athlete himself is the most important factor in the teaching- and learning process. The child, no matter how young and how much of a beginner he may be, is always subject to his own development and never just the object of our influence. Therefore offer them enough tips and opportunities for their own development. Foster and utilize your little shooting athlete's independence. Take the path from directing to inspiring. The children don't have to and aren't supposed to, but they can and they may.

The value of this little book

The value of this little book will depend entirely on how you will integrate it into the instruction. It is written specifically for children who are beginning shooting athletes. But it can also be recommended to parents who wish to accompany their child on this path. The book focuses on the children's needs and is intended to help them also engage in their sport outside of the gym. The child acquires a fairly complete foundation for practicing via the book's illustrations and descriptions. He will be better able to follow your explanations and demonstrations. The children can review at their leisure what they have learned, keep track of goals and learning progress, and receive suggestions for practicing at home and with other children. This develops the ability to act independently and accelerates the learning process

An environment is created in which the children themselves, step by step, think about their practicing and learning, their movements, actions, and finally monitor and evaluate their behavior. They become a partner to the coach and trainer. We would like the children to enjoy coming to practice and go home with a sense of achievement. And of course that would make the practice sessions fun for the trainer as well.

The book and training

Tell the children that this book will be their personal companion as they learn archery, rifle shooting, as well as pistol shooting. Give them the logo of the club and take a photo to paste in the book. This will boost their attachment to you, to the team and the club.

Help the children to use this book properly. In the beginning, read some segments together and explain to the children how the photos and illustrations should be viewed and understood. Make entries regarding goals, suggestions, etc., together. In doing so you create critical orientation guides for their understanding and independent practicing.

With the aid of this book you can also assign homework for the next training session. The children read up on a topic and get to do a show-and-tell at the next session.

We always welcome critical comments and suggestions.

We wish you and your little protégées
lots of fun and enjoyment, and of course
athletic success, too.

Photo & Illustration Credits

Cover design: Sabine Groten
Illustrations: Katrin Barth
Cover photos: © fotolia/Ronald Baumann, © fotolia
Photos (inside):   Berndt Barth, Kathrin Barth, Steffen Däbel, Beate Dreilich, Heiner Köpcke (photo Ralf Schumann), Hans-Jürgen Penquitt, Shooting Sports Organization of Saxony, Ralf Schumann

Illustration on page 17: Val Muntenau from A. Daudet (1979): *The Prodigious Adventures of Tartarin of Tarason*

Novelty targets on page 81 and page 105 by Krüger Schießscheiben